Making Sense of English Grammar

Making Sense of English Grammar

Jake Allsop

CASSELL

CASSELL PUBLISHERS LIMITED
Villiers House, 41–47 Strand
London WC2N 5JE

First published 1989
Reprinted 1990

British Library Cataloguing in Publication Data

Allsop, Jake
    Making sense of English grammar:
    1. English language — Text books for
    foreign speakers
    I. Title
    428.2'4   PE1128
    ISBN 0-304-31292-4

Typeset by Flairplan Ltd, Ware, Herts
Printed in Great Britain at The Bath Press, Avon

Illustrated by Phillip Burrows
Illustration p.87 from Making Sense of Phrasal Verbs, Martin Shovel

Introduction

To the student

You can use a foreign language without learning the rules of its grammar. You can also use a car without learning the traffic code. But you and I will be better drivers if we know and follow the rules of the road. In the same way, you and I will understand each other better if we both follow the traffic rules – the grammar – of the language.

There is more to learning how to drive a car than studying the traffic code, just as there is more to learning a language than studying its grammar. This book, then, is only a part of learning English. But, if you refer to it when you are not sure of something, it will help you to use English well. People will find it easier to listen to you and you will find it easier to say what you mean. You will be a better driver than the person who just got into a car one morning and drove on to the highway.

To the teacher

Those of you who know *Cassell's Students' English Grammar* will recognise a family resemblance. CSEG is widely used by students from intermediate level upwards, and especially by teachers and trainee teachers of English. The present book has been written in response to many requests from CSEG users who feel that their pre-intermediate students would benefit from a CSEG-style grammar at a lower level.

Students want a grammar which will answer their questions without wordy explanations or lists of subtle variations and exceptions. For this reason, the grammar is profusely illustrated, and has a prescriptive tone of voice. I have of course simplified and generalised many things, but without, I hope harmful distortion. The level of this grammar is elementary to lower intermediate, but I have deliberately set the upper limit higher than that label suggests, because we tend to be puzzled more by things on the horizon of our knowledge than by what is close to us.

If your students have this book (with or without your blessing!), you are bound to be affected by it. With this in mind, I have tried to keep a parallel between this book and CSEG in such a way that points dealt with here will be found in a corresponding section of CSEG, where they are, of course, treated in more detail. In this way, you, as teacher, can use CSEG to take your students farther than this grammar goes, when the need arises.

Acknowledgements

Many users of CSEG, both in the UK and overseas, have contributed ideas to this elementary grammar. I thank these good friends and colleagues, too numerous to mention by name. Hermione Ieronymidis read the first draft and made valuable amendments. Throughout the project, I have received a lot of practical help, common sense and moral support from Jenny Tapson. It is to her that this book is dedicated.

Jake Allsop
Cambridge, Summer 1988.

Contents

1 Nouns

1.1 Meaning

A noun answers the question:

▶ Who is it? or What is it?

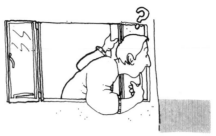

Who is it? or What is it?

Nouns are the names of people, things, places and qualities:

▶ boy, student, house, sky, Italy, love, time, happiness

Nouns can be
— concrete: describing what you can see or touch:
— abstract: describing qualities, ie, what you cannot see or touch:

▶ a woman, a house, the sky, Italy, people

▶ information, love, time, happiness

Concrete nouns can be singular (referring to one) or plural (more than one):

▶

singular	*plural*
a boy, one boy a woman	three boys four women

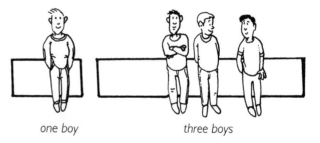

one boy   three boys

Abstract nouns are only singular:

▶ information, happiness

Nouns can be
— countable (count nouns): there can be one or more than one:
— uncountable (mass nouns) they are only in the singular, eg, kinds of food:

▶ a dog, dogs, a cup, cups

▶ bread, cheese, milk, sugar

substances:

▶ grass, soap, snow, water

materials:

▶ cotton, iron, steel, wool

qualities (abstract nouns):

▶ hope, love, sleep, work, happiness

1

These words are mass nouns, and are
only used in the singular:

▶   advice, baggage, furniture, hair, homework, information,
luggage, news, progress, rubbish

Your luggage is in the car.
Your hair looks really nice! What have you done to it?

Your luggage is in the car.

Note that many nouns can be either mass
or count nouns but with a change of
meaning:

mass	count
Windows are made of glass.	I'd like a glass of milk.
Have some more cake!	I've made some cakes for you.
What beautiful hair!	Waiter, there's a hair in my soup.

A noun can be
— one word:

▶   dogs

— a compound (see 1.4):
— a noun phrase:

▶   vacuum cleaner

noun	Dogs	
noun phrase	Dogs with big teeth Stroking big dogs	can be dangerous.

1.2 Form: plurals

To form the plural, add *-s* or *-es* to the singular:

-s	-es
Most nouns: book books seat seat rope ropes car cars	*Nouns ending in -s, -ss, -sh, -ch, -x:* bus buses kiss kisses wish wishes match matches box boxes
Nouns ending in vowel + -y: day days boy boys	*Nouns ending in consonant + -y:* *change y to i* baby babies country countries
Nouns ending in -o: photo photos kilo kilos	*except a few, such as:* potato potatoes tomato tomatoes
Most nouns ending in -fe *change the -f to v:* knife knives wife wives	*Some nouns ending in -f* *change the -f to -v and add -es:* half halves leaf leaves

Irregular plurals include
— these common words: ▶

singular	plural
man	men
woman	women
child	children
foot	feet
tooth	teeth
mouse	mice
sheep	sheep
deer	deer

— some animals which we hunt or eat: ▶

Nouns which are only plural include
— the words *people* and *police:* ▶ There aren't many people here.
The police are looking for a stolen car.

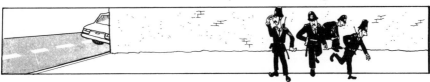

The police are looking for a stolen car.

— tools and clothes which have two parts, eg:

▶ binoculars, glasses, scissors; knickers, pyjamas, shorts, tights, trousers, underpants

Are these your scissors?
These trousers are too short!

These trousers are too short!

Use the word *pair* to talk about more than one:

▶ a pair of glasses
three pairs of underpants

— some common nouns ending in -s eg:

▶ clothes, contents, customs, goods, greetings, surroundings, regards, stairs, thanks

These clothes are very old-fashioned.
My surroundings are very pleasant here.
Christmas greetings are sent in December.

goods

There are some nouns ending in -s which are in fact singular. They include
— some games, sports, and academic subjects, eg:

▶ athletics, billiards, darts, economics, mathematics, physics

Billiards is a difficult game.
Physics is my favourite subject.

— the word *news:*

▶ Bad news travels fast.
No news is good news. (proverb)

With most compound nouns, only the second part becomes plural:

But note
— relatives by marriage, eg:

— some compounds with *man/woman:*

singular	plural
bookshop office block spoonful	bookshops office blocks spoonfuls
brother-in-law woman driver	brothers-in-law women drivers

1.3 Form: male and female

Sometimes there is a different word for male and female, eg:

male	female
bridegroom	bride
brother	sister
father	mother
gentleman	lady
grandfather	grandmother
husband	wife
king	queen
nephew	niece
prince	princess
son	daughter
uncle	aunt
widower	widow

But usually, the same word refers to either a male or a female, eg:

▶ cousin, dentist, doctor, friend, neighbour, nurse, parent, person, scientist, secretary, stranger, student, teacher, typist

Doctors

Other words in the sentence sometimes tell you whether the person is male or female:

▶ My *father* is an art teacher.
The teacher left *her* bag behind.

1.4 Form: compound nouns

Nouns which have two parts are called compound nouns:

▶ post + man   → postman
bed + room   → bedroom
office + block → office block

The second part tells you who or what it is:

▶ a man, a room, a block

The first part tells you what kind it is, or what it is for:

▶ a man who delivers the post
a room where you sleep
a building containing offices

For example:

► a houseboat is a kind of boat
a boathouse is a kind of house

Note that the first part of compound nouns is stressed:

► BEDroom, BOOKshop, POSTman, OFFICE block, SCREWdriver

Write compounds as one word when both parts are short; as two words in other cases:

►

as one word	as two words
bedroom	dining room
bookshop	book exhibition
screwdriver	washing machine

Notice the difference between:

►

a teacup	and	a cup of tea
a milk bottle	and	a bottle of milk
a matchbox	and	a box of matches

a teacup   *a milk bottle*   *a matchbox*   *a cup of tea*   *a bottle of milk*   *a box of matches*

1.5 Form: the possessive

The possessive is a noun phrase in two parts:

► Justine's book, the boys' room

The second part tells you who or what it is:

► a book, a room

The first part tells you who it belongs to, who uses it:

► It belongs to Justine →
It is Justine's book (= her book).
The boys use this room →
It is the boys' room (= their room).

To form the possessive:

Add -'s to the noun					
John Smith	+	's	=	John Smith's	→ John Smith's friends
the cat	+	's	=	the cat's	→ the cat's dinner
a woman	+	's	=	a woman's	→ a woman's work
women	+	's	=	women's	→ women's rights
a child	+	's	=	a child's	→ a child's toy
children	+	's	=	children's	→ children's clothes
If the noun already ends in -s, add -'					
the boys	+	'	=	the boys'	→ the boys' bedroom
ladies	+	'	=	ladies'	→ ladies' fashions
the Smiths	+	'	=	the Smiths'	→ the Smiths' address

the cat's dinner

Many English personal names and surnames end in -s. In these cases, you can add either -'s or -':
The first is easier to pronounce.

▶ Charles's wife or Charles' wife
Mrs Jones's house or Mrs Jones' house

Use the possessive form with
— people, countries and animals:

▶ Men's fashions are not attractive.
Russia's army is the biggest in Europe.
My dog's ears are like silk.

— with expressions of time:

▶ minute, hour, day, month, year
We leave in an hour's time.
I've got two weeks' holiday.
Have you prepared tomorrow's lessons?

— with expressions of place (we often leave out the place):

▶ the doctor's = the doctor's surgery
St Paul's   = St Paul's Cathedral
I must go to the dentist's soon.
We buy all our meat at the butcher's.

We buy all our meat at the butcher's.

In all other cases, we use
— prepositions like *of* and *to*:

▶ the back of the TV set
the pages of a book
the key to the front door
a television programme
a bookshelf
the front door key

— compounds:

2 Determiners I

2.1 Meaning

Determiners are part of a noun phrase. They include:

▶   a/an   the
this/these   that/those
some/any   no/none   (not)much/many
several/a lot of/a little/a few
all/every/each
both/neither/either

Determiners help to
— identify which one(s):

▶   a girl that I know
the boy over there
that house, these cars here

the boy over there

— describe quantity, ie, they tell us
how much or how many:
— describe groups, series and pairs:

▶   some butter, a few cakes
▶   all the boys, every day, each word
both of us, either way

2.2 *a/an*

a/an (the indefinite article) refers to something that you are speaking about for the first time:

▶   I want a book.
Give me an example.

I want a book.

The plural of the noun without an article refers to things in general:
Use *a* before a consonant or consonant sound:

▶   Good books have good examples.

▶   a dog, a French book, a house, a university, a union meeting

Use *an* before a vowel or vowel sound: ▶ an egg, an ugly face
an hour, an honest man*

* The *h* is not pronounced in these words

a/*an* can mean
— a particular one, not named: ▶ They are looking for a man with long hair. He is armed and dangerous.

They are looking for a man with long hair. He is armed and dangerous.

— any one, it doesn't matter which one: ▶ I'm looking for a man to help me with my work.
— one example of a set: ▶ A ruler is an instrument for drawing straight lines.
— *a kind of:* ▶ Polignac is a French brandy.
— X in/for every Y: ▶ two francs a kilo
three times a week

Use *some* as the plural of *a*/*an* for an unspecified number or quantity ▶ I had some boiled eggs for breakfast.
Give me some money!

Use the plural without any article to make general statements: ▶ There are discos in every town.
Dogs make good pets.

Dogs make good pets.

2.3 *the*

the (the definite article) refers to something that you have already spoken about: ▶ Which book do you want?
The book about railways.

Which book do you want? The book about railways.

Pronounced [ðə] before a consonant
or consonant sound: ▶ the dog, the French railways, the University of Bonn

Pronounced [ði:] before a vowel or vowel
sound: ▶ the eggs, the undertaker, the hour

the can mean

— the one(s) you have already referred
to: ▶ They are looking for a man with red hair. The man is
armed and dangerous.

— the one that is well known to
everybody: ▶ The Earth goes round the Sun.
I must go to the bank and the post office.

The Earth goes round the Sun.

— with an adjective, all the people or
things of this kind: ▶ This is a hospital for the blind.
The meaning is plural: the blind = all blind people
The English are fond of tea.

Leave out *the*

— in general plural statements: ▶ Dogs make better pets than horses.

Dogs make better pets than horses.

— in general statements with a mass
noun: ▶ They say sugar is bad for you.

Note: as soon as you go from the general
to the particular, use *the*: ▶ The sugar I like best is Demerara.

What are you talking about?	Children.
What kind of children?	All children.
Do you like children?	I like most children.
What kind of children don't you like?	Noisy children.
Do you know any noisy children?	Yes, *the* children who live next door!

— before the names of particular people: ▶ President Wilson, Admiral Nelson

— continents: ▶ Asia, Africa

— most countries, mountains and lakes with a one-word name: (Use *the* in plural names like *The Netherlands*; and in names with a count noun: *The Red Sea*) ▶ Spain, Mount Everest, Lake Garda

— names of most places in a town: ▶ Times Square, London Bridge, Fleet Street, Abbey Road

— in many fixed expressions such as verb + noun, eg: ▶ take place, have breakfast, make friends, shake hands, make progress, make love

preposition + noun, eg: ▶ for example, after lunch, on time, in turn

Note expressions to describe method of travelling: ▶ go/travel:
by air   by bicycle   by bus
by car   by coach   by plane
by ship   by taxi   by Tube
on foot   on horseback

on foot

by car

There were no buses, so we went on foot.
I enjoy travelling by air.

and expressions like *go to school*, which means to be a pupil, not just to be in a school building: ▶

go	be
to bed	in bed
to church	in church
to hospital	in hospital
to prison	in prison
to town	in town
to school	at school
to sea	at sea
to work	at work
home	at home

For example:

▶ What time do you usually go to bed?

Note the difference between:

▶ He went to prison for stealing a car. = He was a prisoner.

and:

▶ He went to the prison to visit his son. = He was a visitor.

He went to prison.

He went to the prison.

— to save space in such things as headlines:

▶ POLICE SEEK WOMAN IN RED DRESS

— notices:

▶ DO NOT CROSS ROAD

— telegrams, telexes:

▶ MEETING AT TOWN HALL CANCELLED

— diagrams:

▶ BREAK GLASS WITH HAMMER

2.4 *this/these that/those*

this, plural *these*, refers to things near you:

▶ this chair, these days

that, plural *those*, refers to things not near you:

They can stand alone as pronouns:

▶ that chair over there, those old films

▶ What's this?
That's funny. Who did that?
Which are your books? These are.

That's funny. Who did that?

Use the pronoun *one* after *this* and *that* when you are talking about a thing already referred to:

▶ Which is your book? This one.
Which book do you want? That one.

Use *this/these* for things which are
— near you in space: ▶ this apple, these bananas

this apple, these bananas

— near you in time: ▶ this morning, this afternoon, this evening, this week,
this Friday, this July, this month, this year

— inside your personal world: ▶ this street, these houses

this street, these houses

Use *that/those* for things which are
— not near you in space or time: ▶ that man, those people

that man, those people

— outside your personal world: ▶ at that time, in those days

at that time, in those days

3 Determiners II

3.1 Determiners which describe quantity

These determiners are: ▶ much, many, a lot of, some, any, several, a little, a few, much, many, no

They refer to quantities from a lot to nothing. They answer the questions *How much?* (mass nouns) or *How many?* (count nouns):

singular mass nouns	plural count nouns
How much bread is there?	How many loaves are there?
There's a lot of bread.	There are a lot of loaves.
There's some bread.	There are some loaves. There are several loaves.
There isn't much bread. There's a little bread.	There are a few loaves. There aren't many loaves.
There's no bread. There isn't any bread.	There are no loaves. There aren't any loaves.

All these words, except *no*, can stand alone as pronouns (ie, instead of a noun):

▶ How much tea is there?   There's a lot.
I need some money.   Give me some.
Give me some tea.   There isn't any.
How much coffee is there?   Just a little.
How many cups do you need?   Only a few.

no becomes *none:*   ▶ How many cakes are left?   None.

3.2 *some*

Use *some*

— in statements, for an unspecified number or quantity: Count: ▶   I need some envelopes.
                             Mass: ▶   Have some more coffee.

— in questions when you expect the
answer *Yes*:

Did your father give you some money?

▶ Did your father give you some money?
  (I'm sure he gave you some.)

  I haven't got any money.
  Didn't your father give you some?

— in questions when you want to
invite:

▶ Would you like some more coffee?

request:

▶ Could I have some paper, please?

offer:

▶ Shall I put some music on for you?

suggest:

▶ Why don't you do some work?

3.3 *any*

Use *any*
— in negatives:

▶ I haven't got any envelopes.
  There isn't any coffee left.

Also after negative words such as
never, without, hardly:

▶ I never seem to get any letters.
  He did it without any help from me.
  I've had hardly any breakfast.

He did it without any help from me.

— in real questions when you don't
know what the answer will be:

▶ Are there any good theatres in Bristol?
  Did you buy any presents when you were in Spain?

Did you buy any presents?

any also means *it doesn't matter
which one*:

▶ Give me a pen; any pen will do.
  Come and see me any time.

3.4 *no/none*

Use *no* instead of *not . . . any* as the opposite of *some* when you feel very strongly:

▶ I need no help from you!
I have no money to give you.

Use *none* as a one-word answer:

▶ How many have you got left?
None.

3.5 *much/many*

Use *much* for mass and *many* for count objects
— to ask questions:

▶ How much do I owe you?
How many times have you been in a plane?
Do you get much fog in Switzerland?
Are there any wild animals near here?

— with *not,* to form the negative:

▶ Juan doesn't say much,
There aren't many clever people here.

— with *too,* to say that there is/are more than you need:

▶ I can't drink this tea. You've put too much sugar in it.
There are too many chiefs and not enough Indians in this firm!

There are too many chiefs and not enough Indians in this firm!

— with *so* and *as,* to compare:

▶ You shouldn't drink so much coffee or eat so many cakes.
I'll drink as much coffee as I like and eat as many cakes as I like!

Use *much* with *very,* not on its own:

▶ Thank you very much.
I love you very much.

The difference between *some* and *not much/not many* is a question of point of view:

▶ The cupboard is half full — there's still some food left.
The cupboard is half empty — there isn't much food left.

The cupboard is half full.   *The cupboard is half empty.*

3.6 *a lot/a little/a few*

Use *a lot of* for large quantities, and
a little/a few for small quantities:

▶ There's a lot of fruit left: a lot of apples, some grapes and
a few pears.
Shall I put some lipstick on?
OK, but only a little.
Are there many tourists in town?
No, only a few.

Remember to use *a little* with mass
nouns, *a few* with plural count nouns:

▶ We still have a little time left.
I'll be back in a few days.

We still have a little time left.

I'll be back in a few days.

3.7 Compounds *someone, anything*, etc

The words *some, any* and *no* combine
with *-one, -body, -thing* to form
compounds. All are written as one word
except *no one*. The table also includes
the useful compounds with *every*
and *where*:

	one	body	thing	where
some	someone	somebody	something	somewhere
any	anyone	anybody	anything	anywhere
no	no one	nobody	nothing	nowhere
every	everyone	everybody	everything	everywhere

The words ending in *-one* and *-body*
refer to people. There is no difference in
meaning:

▶ There's someone at the door =
There's somebody at the door.

These compounds follow the same
rules as for *some, any* and *no*:

▶ There's something I want to tell you.
Have you anything to say?
Have you something to say? (I think that you have.)
I couldn't find anyone to come with me.
They never tell me anything!

Use the *no-* compounds
— in one-word answers:

▶ Where have you been? Nowhere.
Who have you been with? Nobody.
What have you been doing? Nothing.

Where have you been? Nowhere.   *Who have you been with? Nobody.*   *What have you been doing? Nothing.*

— as subject:

▶ Nobody knows the trouble I've seen.
Nothing acts faster than Alka Seltzer.

— when you feel strongly:

▶ I will tell you nothing!

I will tell you nothing!

Note the difference between:

▶ Who invented the telephone?
Anybody (= everybody) knows that.

and:

▶ Who invented the wheel?
Nobody knows that.

4 Determiners III

4.1 Determiners which describe groups

all, every, each, both, either and *neither* are used to describe groups:

3 or more in a group	all every
2 or more in a group	each
2 in a group (= a pair)	both either neither

Use *all* and *both* to **join**, ie, you see the group as one thing:

▶ All my students are clever.
Both roads lead to London.

All my students are clever.

Use *each, every, either* and *neither* to **separate**, ie, you see the group as a number of individual things:

▶ Every student in my class is clever.
I shall give each of them a present.
Both roads lead to London. You can take either road; neither of them goes through Birmingham.

each   *every*

The meaning of *all, every* and *each* is very similar. Use the word which best describes how you look at things.

Both roads lead to London.
Neither of them goes through Birmingham.

4.2 *all*

All is used in these combinations:

With plural count noun	
all (the)* *all these/those* *all my, etc*	All the tourists had cameras. All those books belong to Linda. All my friends can speak English.
With mass noun (singular)	
all (the)* *all this/that* *all my, etc*	Have you been here all the time? Who has made all this mess? All our work has been in vain.

* Leave out *the*
— in general statements:

▶ All passengers must fasten their seatbelts.
   All information is confidential.

— in time expressions, eg:

▶ all day, all night, all morning, all week
   It took us all week to finish the job.

But note:
You can say *all of the/this/these/that/those/my*, etc, usually to compare with *some of, none of*, etc:

▶ all the time

▶ All of the tourists had cameras. Some of them had Nikons, but none of them had Canons.

There are two ways of using *all* with pronouns:
— pronoun + *all*:

▶ We all need to be loved.
   God bless you all!
   They have all passed their exams.

— *all of* + pronoun:

▶ All of us need to be loved.
   God bless all of you!
   How many have passed? All of them.

Use *all* on its own
— when it means *the only thing*:

▶ All I want is a quiet life.
   All we need now is a long holiday.

All I want is a quiet life.

— in the expression *not . . . at all*:

▶ I don't like him at all.
We haven't done any work at all.

— in the expression *Not at all!*:

▶ Thank you very much!
Not at all! = You're welcome! or Don't mention it!

Use *everything/everybody* instead of *all*
in other cases:

▶ Everything I've told you is true.
Give everybody a copy of the report.

4.3 *every*

Every is used in these combinations:

every + singular count noun	I checked every answer: they were all wrong.
every + pronoun *one*	I looked at the answers: every one was wrong.
every one of + plural noun	I checked every one of the answers.
every one of + pronoun	I checked every one of them.

Use *every* to describe things which you
see as a series:

▶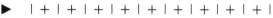

Use *all* to describe the same series
seen as a group:

▶

This is a football team.

All the players are fit.

Every one of them is fit.

This is a library.

All the books are numbered.

Every book is numbered.

Use *every*, not *all*, in expressions of regular time:

▶ I go shopping every Saturday.
She buys new clothes every Spring.
Every time I see him, I start laughing.

4.4 *each*

Each is used in these combinations:

each + singular count noun	Take each day as it comes. (popular saying)
each + pronoun *one*	I picked up the letters and examined each one very carefully.
each + *other*	We love each other very much.
each of + plural noun	He gave each of the boys a present.
each of + pronoun	He gave each of them a present.

Use *each*
— to point to the individual things in a
   group of two or more:

▶ I have checked every book on the subject, and I find that each one says something different.
He said hello to all the children, and then gave each one of them a present.

— in the pattern quantity + *each* :

▶ How much are the oranges? 15 pence each.
He had six left, so he gave them three each.

4.5 *both* and *either/neither*

These words refer to a group of two, ie, a pair. Use *both* to **join**; use *either* to **separate**:

▶ Have both cakes!
both cakes = cake A *and* cake B
You get two cakes!

Have both cakes!

▶ Have either cake!
either cake = cake A *or* cake B
You get one cake!

Have either cake!

Both is used in these combinations:

both (the)		I went to both (the) concerts.
both these/those	+ plural noun	Both these books belong to me.
both my, etc		Both our children are at school.

The verb after *both* should be in the plural.
You can put *of* after *both,* with little change of meaning:

▶ Both of these books belong to me.

There are two ways of using *both* with pronouns:

| *both of* + pronoun | : |

▶ Both of us like sunbathing.
I have two cats, and I hate both of them.

I have two cats, and I hate both of them.

| pronoun + *both* | : |

▶ We both like sunbathing.
I have two cats, and I hate them both.

Either/neither is used in these combinations. All these forms have the same meaning:

either	Both roads lead to the centre. You can take either.
either + singular count noun	Take either road.
either + pronoun *one*	Take either one.
either of + plural noun	Take either of the roads.
either of + pronoun	Take either of them.

The verb after *either* should be in the singular:

▶ Either road takes you there.
Either of the roads takes you there.

Use *neither*
— as the subject of the sentence:

▶ Neither dress really suits you.
Neither of them said a word.

Neither dress really suits you.

— as a short answer:

▶ Which one do you like?
Neither.
Neither of them.

— in expressions like
So do I/Neither do I
to show that you agree with
speaker:

▶   'I like pasta.' 'So do I.'

'I like pasta.' 'So do I.'

'I don't like Alan.' 'Neither does his boss.'
'John can't swim.' 'Neither can his wife.'

In other cases, use *not . . . either*:

▶   I have two blue dresses, but I don't like either of them.
(instead of '. . . but I like neither of them.')

Similarly with other negatives, like
never, without, hardly:

▶   He left without speaking to either of them.

5 Adjectivals

5.1 Meaning

Adjectivals are words which say
something more about a noun. They
identify the one you are talking about.
They answer the question: ▶   Which one? or Which ones?

Which one?   *Which ones?*

5.2 Form

They can be
— single words (adjectives):   ▶

a	good	man
the	next	day
two	difficult	questions

— phrases, often with the pattern
preposition + noun: ▶

	prep.	noun
the best man	in	the world
the day	after	the race

or participle + noun: ▶

	part.	noun
two questions	needing	an answer

— clauses with a main verb and
introduced by *who, which, whose* or
that: ▶

noun phrase	adjectival clause	
This is the man	who	loves me.
This is the man	(that)	I love.
I have a car	that / which	uses methane.
Is that the man	whose	car you hit?

In sentences like this the clause does
not identify the noun phrase (*Saturn*),
but simply adds some more
information: ▶   I want to talk about Saturn,
which is a very interesting planet.

5.3 Word order

Most adjectives come immediately
before the noun. Other words, such as
all, some, etc come first:

some of	the	last	few		
both	this/these	next	lot of		
either of	that/those	other	one	adjective	noun
all	my, your, etc	first	two		
half	John's	second	three		
		etc	etc		

For example: ▶   all these other difficult words
the first few English lessons
my other two cotton dresses

If there is more than one adjective,
the order is usually:

quality	size	age/heat	shape	colour	origin	material
beautiful	big	old		blue		iron
nice	little	young	square	red	French	cotton
important	small	modern	round	white	Victorian	metal
dirty	light	cold		dark	urban	plastic
tall	huge	hot		green		nylon

For example: ▶   an ugly old house
a tall young man
a new red London bus

A few adjectives do not come before a
noun but only after a verb like *be, seem,
look, feel, taste, smell, sound, appear,
become, get:*   ▶   afraid, alike, alone, ashamed, asleep, awake, content, glad,
ill, well

You don't look very well. Are you ill?
I'm glad you came to see me.
I was ashamed of myself.
You seem tired
I feel angry,
It tastes good.

5.4 Comparisons

Use these forms to compare two or more things:

▶

small	smaller	smallest
useful	more useful	most useful

There are three patterns.
When two things are equal, use.
as . . . as:

▶ A is   as small as   B.

When two things are not equal, use
-er than or *more* adjective *than*:

▶ A is   smaller than   B.
   A is   more intelligent than B.

To compare one thing with two or
more other things, use *the -est of/in*:
or *the most* adjective *of/in*:

▶ A is the smallest of them all.
▶ A is the most intelligent in the class.

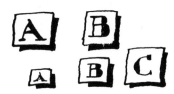

A is smaller than B
A is the smallest in the group

Add *-(e)r* and *-(e)st* to
— one-syllable adjectives:

▶

sad	sadder	saddest
brave	braver	bravest

— two-syllable adjectives ending in
-le, -ly, -ow and *-er:*

▶

simple	simpler	simplest
lovely	lovelier	loveliest

— other two-syllable adjectives eg:

▶ common, handsome, pleasant, quiet

Note these adjectives, which are
irregular:

▶

bad / ill	worse	worst
far	farther / further	farthest / furthest
good / well	better	best
little	less	least
much/many	more	most

Use *more* and *most*
with all other adjectives:
If you are not sure of which form to
use, use *more/most*:

▶

▶

selfish	more selfish	most selfish
polite	more polite	most polite
tired	more tired	most tired

5.5 Patterns with adjectives

make + person + adjective:

▶ He made me very angry.
Unripe fruit will make you ill.

It is *adjective* (for someone) to do:

▶ It is too heavy for me to carry.
It must be hard to learn Japanese.

It is too heavy for me to carry.

Other verb + adjective patterns are:

▶ come true
fall asleep, fall ill
feel/look/sound ill, tired, etc
get angry, get better, etc
go bad, go mad, go stale
grow old
keep quiet
make sure
sit/stand still
turn blue, red, etc
Lisa's fallen asleep in class again!
Your nose has turned blue.

Note the meaning of adjectives ending in *-ing* or *-ed*:

▶ boring   bored
interesting   interested
exciting   excited

X is exciting = X excites me
X is exciting, so I am excited
What an interesting picture: I am very interested in modern painting.

What an interesting picture! I am very interested in modern painting.

5.6 Nationalities

There are several different endings: ▶

-ese	Chinese, Japanese
-n/-an/-ian	Cuban, German, Canadian
ish	Danish, Spanish
-ch	Dutch, French
-i	Iraqi, Israeli

Note also: Greek, Swiss

The word for the people is usually the same as the adjective: ▶

adjective	a citizen	the people
Portuguese	a Portuguese	the Portuguese
Indian	an Indian	the Indians
Kuwaiti	a Kuwaiti	the Kuwaitis

But sometimes it is different: ▶

British	a Briton	the British
Danish	a Dane	the Danes
Finnish	a Finn	the Finns
Polish	a Pole	the Poles
Scottish	a Scot	the Scots
Spanish	a Spaniard	the Spanish
Swedish	a Swede	the Swedes
Turkish	a Turk	the Turks

Add *-man/-men* or *woman/women* to: ▶

Dutch	a Dutchman	the Dutch
English	an Englishman	the English
French	a Frenchman	the French
Irish	an Irishman	the Irish
Welsh	a Welshman	the Welsh

A Dutchman, an Englishman and two Frenchmen were having a discussion.

Always write nationality adjectives with a capital letter: ▶ I like Danish beer, German sausage, French wine and Italian pasta.

I like French wine and Italian pasta

5.7 Numbers

The numbers *one, two, three*, etc. answer
the question: ▶   How many?
The numbers *first, second, third*, etc,
answer the question: ▶   In what order?
Take care with the spelling of the
underlined numbers:

0 zero/nought			
1 one	1st first	21 twenty-one	21st twenty-first
2 two	2nd second	22 twenty-two	22nd twenty-second
3 three	3rd third	23 twenty-three	23rd twenty-third
4 four	4th fourth	24 twenty-four	24th twenty-fourth
5 five	5th fifth	30 thirty	30th thirtieth
6 six	6th sixth	40 forty	40th fortieth
7 seven	7th seventh	50 fifty	50th fiftieth
8 eight	8th eighth	60 sixty	60th sixtieth
9 nine	9th ninth	70 seventy	70th seventieth
10 ten	10th tenth	80 eighty	80th eightieth
11 eleven	11th eleventh	90 ninety	90th ninetieth
12 twelve	12th twelfth	100 one hundred	100th hundredth
13 thirteen	13th thirteenth	101st hundred and one	101 hundred and first
14 fourteen	14th fourteenth	200 two hundred	200th two hundredth
15 fifteen	15th fifteenth	1000 one thousand	1000th thousandth
16 sixteen	16th sixteenth	2000 two thousand	2000th two thousandth
17 seventeen	17th seventeenth	3,400 three thousand four hundred	
18 eighteen	18th eighteenth	1,000,000 one million	1,000,000th one millionth
19 nineteen	19th nineteenth	2,000,000 two million	
20 twenty	20th twentieth		

Note how we express the following:
— the date: ▶   21st May, 21 May or May 21 =
                                             May the twenty-first, or
                                             the twenty-first of May

— the year   ▶   1992 =
                                             nineteen ninety-two

— telephone numbers: ▶   012-77003 =
                                             oh one two double seven double oh three

6 Pronouns

6.1 Meaning

Pronouns refer to people or things.

People:	▶	I/we/you/he/she/*they*
Things:	▶	it/they

I   you   he   she   it

6.2 Form

In most cases, there is a different form for subject and object: ▶

*Always with a capital letter ▶

	singular		*plural*	
	subject	*object*	*subject*	*object*
	I*	me	we	us
	you	you	you	you
	he	him		
	she	her	they	they
	it	it		

6.3 Uses

He refers to males:
She refers to females:
It refers to things and to animals:

▶ Who's John?   He's my brother.
▶ Who's Mary?   She's my sister.
▶ What's that?   It's a corkscrew.
Is that a horse in striped pyjamas?
No, it's a zebra.

Use he/she for animals only when the sex is known or important to you:
Use the subject pronouns I/we/you/he/she/it/they before the verb: ▶

▶ This is my cat. She's a Persian.

▶ I live in Cambridge.
We have a big house in the centre.
You look very tired.
He isn't here today.
They are outside.

Use it
— to talk about the weather:

▶ It's a lovely day, isn't it?
It's raining/snowing/windy/sunny.
It looks cold outside.

— to talk about the time:

▶ It's twelve o'clock.
It's the first of June today.

— in some common patterns:

▶ It's nice to see you.
It was difficult for me to understand her.
It's a pity/shame you couldn't come.

Use *they* to mean *people in authority*: ▶ They're going to put up prices again.
Use *you* to mean *people in general*: ▶ You can never find a taxi when you want one.

You can never find a taxi when you want one.

Use the object pronouns *me/us/you/ him/ her/it/them*
— after the verb: ▶ Janet has two children and she loves them both.
I didn't see him or her.
Please help us!
Take these books and put them in the cupboard.

— after prepositions: ▶

	prep	object pronoun
Look	at	me.
You can go	with	them.
Don't leave	without	it/one.
Are these	for	us?

— in one-word answers: ▶ Who wants an ice-cream? Me!
Who broke the window? Not me!

Who broke the window? Not me!

Note that *there* is a kind of pronoun in the pattern | *There's a/some/etc* : | ▶ There's a fly in my soup.
There's a lot of traffic on the roads.

6.4 Indirect object pronouns

Some verbs have two objects:

▶ ask, bring, buy, fetch, get, give, hand, lend, make, pass, send, show, teach, tell, write

Use the object pronouns to express the indirect object:

▶

verb	indirect object	direct object
Give	me	a kiss.
I told	her	the truth.
I didn't ask	him	his name.
Did you bring	us	any food?
I want to teach	you	a song.
They're buying	her	a dog.

If both objects are pronouns, you can use either of these patterns:

▶ Give me it. *or* Give it to me.
Bring us it. *or* Bring it to us.

If you are not sure, use the second pattern:

▶

verb	dir obj	to
Lend	it	to her.

You must use the second pattern with these verbs:

▶ explain, mention, say

Please explain	it	to me.
I'll mention	it	to her.
Did he say	anything	to you?

6.5 Possessives

The possessives *my/mine*, etc, answer the question:

▶ Whose is it? Whose are they?

They are:

subject	adjective	pronoun
I	my	mine
he	his	his
she	her	hers
it	its	its
we	our	ours
you	your	yours
they	their	theirs

Use the adjectives with a noun; use the pronouns on their own:

▶ Is that his book? No, it's hers.
Whose car is that outside? Is it yours?

Use a possessive adjective, not *the*, when you are talking about parts of the body, clothes, etc:

▶ I've hurt my arm.
Have you washed your hair lately?
They put on their coats.
She's lost her handbag.

Use *own* with a possessive adjective to make it clear that something belongs to one person and not to another:

▶ It's her own flat. = She bought it.

6.6 Reflexives

The reflexive pronouns, *myself*, etc, show that the subject and object are the same:

▶ She hurt herself.
Did you enjoy yourselves?

Take care with the form of the underlined pronouns:

▶

singular	plural
myself	ourselves
yourself	yourselves
himself	
herself	themselves
itself	

Use reflexives
— when subject and object are the same:

▶ The children behaved themselves.

— after verb + preposition:

▶ She doesn't look after herself.
Take care of yourself.

— after *by* to mean *alone*:

▶ He lives by himself. = alone
I made it all by myself. = without help

He lives by himself.

I made it all by myself.

— to make it clear that you do not mean someone else:

▶ What a pretty dress? Did your mother make it for you?
No, I made it myself.

6.7 *one/ones*   *other/others*   *another/one another*

Use the pronoun *one(s)* instead of a count noun already referred to:

▶ Do you want a blue pen or a black one?
Sell the small chairs, but keep the big ones.

Do not use *one* instead of a mass noun:
▶ Some people like French wine; others prefer Italian.

Use the pronoun *other(s)* instead of a count noun already referred to in contrast to *one* or *some*:

▶ Ann bought two folders. She gave one to Michael and kept the other.
Some like French; others prefer Italian.

Note that *an + other* is written as one word:

▶ another
I've already had one drink; I don't want another.

Use *one another* or *each other* to show that A ⇆ B:

▶ They love each other very much.
Be nice to one another.

Note the difference between *each other/ one another* and *. . . selves*:

▶ They smiled at each other.
They smiled at themselves.

They smiled at each other A ⇄ B

They smiled at themselves A ↔ A, B ↔ B

6.8 Relative pronouns

These are:

	subject	object	possessive
People	who	whom	whose
Things	which	which	—
People or things	that	that	—

Examples of subject pronouns:

▶ I'm just a girl who can't say 'No'.
                         that
  I hate cars which make a loud noise.
                    that

We usually leave out the object pronoun:

▶ You're the girl I really love.
  Paris is a city we visit quite often.

even when it is the object of a preposition:

▶ That's the man the police are looking for (Rather than *That's the man for whom the police are looking.*)
  It's not a subject I know much about. (Rather than *It's not a subject about which I know much.*)

Example of the possessive form:

▶ Are you the man whose daughter painted all these wonderful pictures?

Do not use *whose* for things. Use *of which* or some other construction:

▶ We have an old house the roof of which is made of straw. (*or* We have an old house, and its roof is made of straw.)

7 Prepositions

7.1 Meaning

Prepositions show how things relate to each other in space, time, or in other ways.

Space:

▶ Where?
He lived *in* a small village *near* Lille.
Put your coat *on* the chair.

Time:

▶ When?
Let's meet *after* work.
I haven't seen her *for* a long time.

Purpose:

▶ Why?
I only did it *for* the money.

Method:

▶ How?
He opened the tin *with* a knife.
We went *by* train.

Possession:

▶ A is part *of* B.
the top *of* the hill
the leg *of* the chair

7.2 Preposition + object

Prepositions are followed by a noun or noun phrase:

▶

	prep.	*noun phrase*
We went	on	foot.
It was	under	the chair.
Do it	after	ten o'clock.
Look	at	that!

With pronouns, use the object form:

▶

Walk	towards	me.
Sit	between	John and me.

But remember reflexives:

▶

Look	after	yourself.
I did it	by	myself.

With verbs, use the gerund:

▶

He's good	at	typing.
I'm tired	of	waiting.
I'm not used	to*	studying.

* (Note that *to* can be part of the infinitive, as in *I want to go*.)
With verbs which are followed by a preposition, note that the preposition comes at the end
— in questions:

▶ What are you looking at?
Who does this belong to?

— in relative clauses which identify:

▶ This is the book I was talking about.
Show me the restaurant you went to.

7.3 Prepositions referring to space

The commonest of these are:

▶ above, across, against, along, among, at, away, from, behind, below, between, by, down, from, in, in front of, inside, into, near, next to, off, on, opposite, out of, over, past, round, through, to, towards, under, up

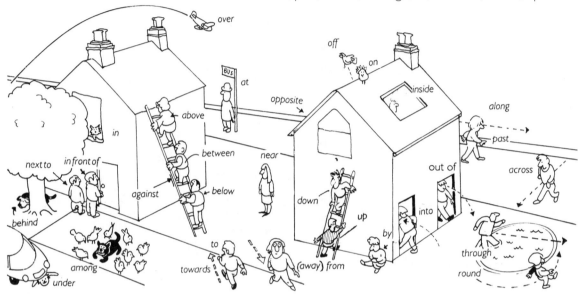

in and *at*
Note the difference between *in* and *at*. Use *at* when it is not important to say exactly where the person/thing is. Use *in* when you want to be exact:

▶ The children were at home all day. = not at school
The children are in the house. = not in the garden
We stayed at the Crest hotel.
It was raining so we stayed in the hotel.
The plane arrived at London airport.
I will be in London tomorrow.

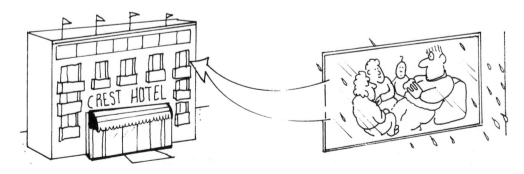

We stayed at the Crest hotel.   *It was raining so we stayed in the hotel.*

in, into and *inside*

Use *into* to make clear the idea of
moving or entering:

▶ He jumped into the river.
Don't go into the forest alone.
I looked into his eyes.

Compare these two sentences:

▶ We walked into the park.
We walked in the park.

We walked into the park.

We walked in the park.

Inside is more precise than *in*;
it always refers to an enclosed space:

▶ Stay inside the house: there is a lion in the garden!

Stay inside the house: there is a lion in the garden!

over/under and *above/below*

Use *over/under* when you want to relate
things vertically:

▶ A is over B
B is under A

Use *above/below* when one thing is
higher than another:

▶ A is above B
B is below A

near and next to
Use *near* when objects are in the same general space:
Use *next to* when objects are side by side:

▶ The cinema is near the grocer's.

▶ The grocer's is next to the butcher's.

opposite and against
Use *opposite* when things are facing each other:
Use *against* when objects are touching or pushing each other:

▶ The cinema is opposite the cafe.

▶ The boy was leaning against the wall.

The boy was leaning against the wall.

between and among
Use *between* for two things or sets of things:

▶ Newport is between Bristol and Cardiff.
The football final will be between Manchester United and Arsenal.

Use *among* for groups or crowds of things:

▶ I found a love letter among my papers.
It is nice to be among friends.

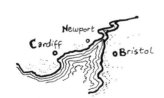

Newport is between Bristol and Cardiff.

It is nice to be among friends.

7.4 Prepositions referring to time

The commonest of these are:

▶ after, at, before, during, for, from, in, on, past, since, to, until (till)

to and *past*
Use these to tell the time:

▶

three o'clock   ten past three

quarter past three   half past three

twenty to four   quarter to four

Note also:
at

▶ at the weekend
at night
at midnight/noon/midday/three o'clock

on
Use *on* with days and dates, eg:

▶ on Friday, on Fridays
on Friday morning/afternoon/evening/night
on March the first   *or*
on the first of March

in
Use *in* with months, seasons and years ▶

in July, in 1988
in (the) spring, in (the) summer
in (the) autumn, in (the) winter

and with parts of the day:

▶ in the morning, in the afternoon, in the evening
(*but*: at night)

by
By means not later than:

▶ Will you finish before 6 o'clock?
I'm not sure, but I'll certainly finish by 7. = not later than 7

until (or *till*)
Use *until* for a period of time which starts now and stops at a point in the future:

▶ Stay here until seven thirty.
We cannot leave till Saturday.

during
During means after the start and before the finish:

▶ We met during the war.
Do not smoke during the concert.

since and *for*
Use these words to talk about a period of time starting in the past. Use *since* to show the starting point of the action:

▶ David has lived here since January.

Use *for* to show the length of time of the action:

▶ David has lived here for three months.

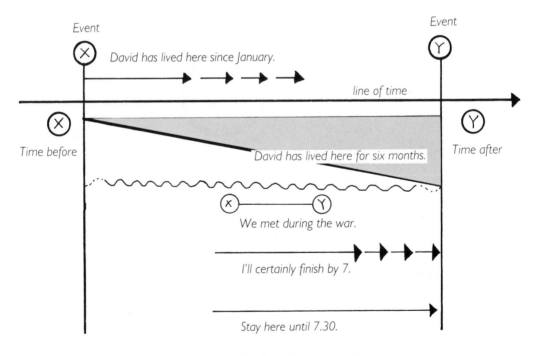

Event

Event

David has lived here since January.

line of time

Time before

David has lived here for six months.

Time after

We met during the war.

I'll certainly finish by 7.

Stay here until 7.30.

Read the diagrams in this way:
Since *a point of time, ie, starting from that point.*
For *a period of time, ie, starting at ⊗ and finishing at Ⓨ.*
During *a period of time, but not necessarily for the whole period.*
By *a point of time, ie, not later than Ⓨ, and perhaps before.*
Until *a point of time, ie, stopping only when that point is reached.*

7.5 Prepositions describing other relationships

The commonest of these are:

▶ about, according to, against, at, by, except, for, from, in spite of, instead of, like, of, than, with, without

Examples:

about:

▶ He wrote a book about birds.
What are you talking about?

according to:

▶ According to our records, you owe us £2,000.

against:

▶ I'm against racist propaganda.

at:

▶ Are you laughing at me?

by:

▶ He left by the back door.

You cannot start a car by kicking it.
Oliver Twist is a novel by Dickens.

except:

▶ We won every match except one.

for:

▶ I'm for (= in favour of) freedom of speech.

from:

▶ I come from Barcelona.
He makes model cars from (= out of) matchboxes.

in spite of:

▶ We went for a walk in spite of the rain.

instead of:

▶ Why don't you do something instead of just talking?

like:

▶ She smokes like a chimney.
It looks like chicken but it tastes like plastic.

of:

▶ This plate is made of silver.
This soup tastes of soap.

than: ·

▶ When you are thirsty, tea is better than coffee.

with:

▶ Cut the string with a knife!
(= use a knife to cut the string.)
Come with me!

Cut the string with a knife!

without:

▶ Do you always go to bed without getting undressed?

7.6 Fixed expressions

There are many expressions with prepositions. The commonest are:

▶

verb + preposition	
account for	look after
accuse someone of	look at
agree with	look for
apologise for	look forward to
approve of	look like
arrive at	long for
ask for	object to
be/get used to	pay for
believe in	prevent from
belong to	rely on
blame someone for	reply to
borrow from	see to
come from	separate A from B
congratulate s/o on	stare at
depend on	suffer from
(wouldn't) dream of	take after
escape from	talk about
exchange A for B	tell A from B
get rid of	tell someone about
hope for	thank someone for
laugh at	think about/of
listen to	worry about

adjective + preposition

absent from	grateful for
accustomed to	guilty of
afraid of	happy about
angry about	interested in
anxious about	jealous of
ashamed of	keen on
aware of	late for
bad at	married to
bad for	new to
close to	pleased with
different from	proud of
disappointed with	ready for
due to	responsible for
excited about	sad about
familiar with	satisfied with
famous for	similar to
fond of	sorry about
full of	sorry for
glad about	sure about
good at	tired of
good for	

preposition + noun phrase

at breakfast	in a hurry	on fire
at dinner/lunch	in bed	on foot
at first	in church	on holiday
at home	in difficulties	on leave
at last	in fact	on purpose
at least	in general	on the contrary
at once	in half	on the other hand
at school	in hospital	on time
at times	in love	out of breath
at work	in order	out of control
by accident	in practice	out of danger
by air, train, bus, etc	in prison	out of date
by chance	in private	out of order
by heart	in public	out of sight
by mistake	in time	to/into hospital
by name	in trouble	to church
by sight	in turns	to court
for ever	in vain	to prison
for example	on average	to school
for good	on board	
for sale	on business	

8 Introduction to verbs

8.1 Meaning

Verbs describe actions or states.
Actions may be physical: ▶ play, sleep, eat, work, drive, live

or mental: ▶ think, dream, look forward, worry

Some people work to live, others live to work.
I am looking forward to seeing you.

States are described by such verbs as: ▶ be, look, seem, appear, contain

You look very sad; are you all right?

You look very sad; are you all right?

8.2 Tenses

The meaning of every verb form has two parts:
1 The time when the action happens.
2 Our view of the action (= our attitude).

The time of the action may be
— the present: ▶ I wonder.
It's raining.

— the past: ▶ He left.
She was sleeping.

— the future: ▶ She'll be here later.
It's going to rain.

Our view of the action may be
— that it is unfinished (we see only a part of it): ▶ John's writing a computer program.
She was sleeping when I arrived.

John's writing a computer program.

— that it is finished (we see the whole action): ▶ John has written a computer program.
Maria fell asleep in class yesterday.

John has written a computer program.

— that we are sure or unsure about
what will happen:

▶ It will rain later.

It's going to rain.

It may rain later.

8.3 Form

Regular verbs have only four parts: ▶

form	example
talk	I/We/You/They talk.
	I want to talk.
talks	He/She talks a lot.
	I have a parrot that talks.
talking	He is talking to someone.
	I'm tired of talking.
talked	They talked all night.
	Have you talked to her yet?

There are two 'simple' tenses, present
and past: ▶

Present	I/We/You/They talk.
	He/She/It talks.
Past	I/We/You/They talked.
	He/She/It

The parts *talk, talking, talked* combine
with parts of *be* and *have* to make the
other tenses: ▶

Continuous	Gianni is learning English.
Passive	My dog is called Spot.
Perfect	We have talked enough.

They also combine with these words,
called modals, to express many other
ideas:

▶
will/would	may/might
shall/should	must/have to
can/could	need
used to	ought to

For example:

▶ Will you let me help you?
They would like to stay here.
I can speak French.
You ought to be in bed.

8.4 Regular and irregular verbs

Regular verbs form the past simple
and the past participle by adding *-d* if the
verb ends in *-e,* or *-ed* in other cases: ▶

base	*past*	*past participle*
move talk	moved talked	moved talked

There are about 100 common verbs
which form the past simple and past
participle differently. For example: ▶

take send	took sent	taken sent

The two most important are *be* and *have*:

be	I	he/she/it	we/you/they	participles
Present	am	is	are	being
Past	was		were	been
Perfect	have been	has been	have been	having been
Future	will be			

have	I	he/she/it	we/you/they	participles
Present	have	has	have	having
Past	had			had
Perfect	have had	has had	have had	having had
Future	will have			

The other common irregular verbs are:

base	past	past participle
beat	beat	beaten
become	became	become
begin	began	begun
bend	bent	bent
bite	bit	bitten
blow	blew	blown
break	broke	broken
bring	brought	brought
build	built	built
burst	burst	burst
buy	bought	bought
catch	caught	caught
choose	chose	chosen
come	came	come
cost	cost	cost
cut	cut	cut
dig	dug	dug
do	did	done
draw	drew	drawn
drink	drank	drunk
drive	drove	driven
eat	ate	eaten
fall	fell	fallen
feel	felt	felt
fight	fought	fought
find	found	found
fly	flew	flown
forget	forgot	forgotten
forgive	forgave	forgiven
freeze	froze	frozen
get	got	got
give	gave	given
go	went	gone
grow	grew	grown
hear	heard	heard
hide	hid	hidden
hit	hit	hit
hold	held	held
hurt	hurt	hurt
keep	kept	kept
know	knew	known
lead	led	led
leave	left	left
lend	lent	lent
let	let	let
lie	lay	lain
light	lit	lit

base	past	past participle
lose	lost	lost
make	made	made
mean	meant	meant
meet	met	met
may	paid	paid
put	put	put
read	read	read
ride	rode	ridden
ring	rang	rung
rise	rose	risen
run	ran	run
say	said	said
see	saw	seen
sell	sold	sold
send	sent	sent
set	set	set
sew	sewed	sewn
shake	shook	shaken
shine	shone	shone
shoot	shot	shot
show	showed	shown
shut	shut	shut
sing	sang	sung
sit	sat	sat
sleep	slept	slept
speak	spoke	spoken
spend	spent	spent
stand	stood	stood
steal	stole	stolen
stick	stuck	stuck
swear	swore	sworn
swim	swam	swum
take	took	taken
teach	taught	taught
tear	tore	torn
tell	told	told
think	thought	thought
throw	threw	thrown
wake	woke	woken
wear	wore	worn
win	won	won
write	wrote	written

8.5 Question and negative forms

Questions

In a question, the subject and the verb in
position 2 change places:

1	2	3
subject	(be, have or modal)	verb
It	is	raining.
John	can	swim.
They	have	left.

2	1	3
(be, have or modal)	subject	verb
Is	it	raining?
Can	John	swim?
Have	they	left?

Where there is nothing in position 2, ie
in the present and past simple, put in
part of *do* (*do, does, did*).

The main verb (*talks, drinks, answered*)
goes back to the base form:

1	2	3
They		talk.
She		drinks.
He		answered.
We		went.

2	1	3
Do	they	talk?
Does	she	drink?
Did	he	answer?
Did	we	go?

Negatives

To make a sentence negative, put the
word *not* after the verb in position 2:

1	2	3
It	is	raining.
He	has	gone.

1	2	not	3
It	is	not	raining.
He	has	not	gone.

In the case of the simple tenses, put in a
part of *do* (*do, does, did*):

1	2	3
They		talk.
She		drinks.
He		answered.
We		went.

1	2	not	3
They	do	not	talk.
She	does	not	drink.
He	did	not	answer.
We	did	not	go.

8.6 Short forms

These verbs have short forms:

▶
am	→ 'm	I'm very happy.
is	→ 's	John's a fool.
has	→ 's	She's got a cold.
have	→ 've	They've gone away.
are	→ 're	We're students.
had	→ 'd	She'd already left.
would	→ 'd	I'd like a cup of tea.
should	→ 'd	I'd like a cup of tea.
will	→ 'll	I'll see you later.

To form the negative, you can add *not*: ▶   I'm not very happy.
John's not a fool.

In the case of *am*, you must say:
In other cases, the commoner way to
form the negative is to shorten *not* to
n't and add it to the verb:

▶   I'm not ...

▶
is not	→ isn't
are not	→ aren't
was not	→ wasn't
were not	→ weren't
has not	→ hasn't
have not	→ haven't
had not	→ hadn't
do not	→ don't
does not	→ doesn't
did not	→ didn't

You can also add *n't* to the modals: ▶   mustn't, shouldn't, etc
Note these special forms: ▶   can + not → cannot *or* can't
will + not → won't
shall + not → shan't

Use the short forms
— in speaking: ▶   Hi, how's it going? I haven't seen you for ages.
— in informal writing (eg personal
   letters):

▶
> Dear Bill,
> I've been on holiday.
> That's why I haven't
> written to you lately...

— to make negative questions: ▶   Why don't you go out more often?
Isn't he Ramon's brother?

— in question tags: ▶   You're Ramon's brother, aren't you?
It's a lovely day, isn't it?

— in short answers: ▶   Does Bill live here?
No, he doesn't.

9 Simple and continuous forms

9.1 Present simple: *I talk, he listens*

The present simple is formed as follows:

▶

I/We/ You/They	talk. don't talk.	
He/She/It	talks. doesn't talk.	
Do	I/we/you/they	talk?
Does	he/she/it	talk?

Note that *do* and *go* add *-es:*

▶ I do → he does   I go → he goes

Meaning:

▶

Time:	not important, any time
Attitude:	we are interested in the fact of the action, not the time.

Use the present simple
— to make general true statements:

▶ The Earth goes round the Sun.
Money doesn't buy happiness.

— to describe your everyday life:

▶ I live and work in Cambridge.
My brother makes more money than I do.

— for things that depend on a fixed timetable or plan:

▶ The London coach leaves in five minutes' time.
She starts her new job next week.

Use the present simple with verbs which refer to
— opinion, feelings, mental states, eg: ▶ believe, care, expect, feel, forget, hate, imagine, know, like, love, mean, mind, notice, prefer, regret, remember, suggest, suppose, think, understand, want, wish

I think you're crazy.
What does 'fragile' mean?

— possession, eg:

▶ belong, have (or have got), own, possess

This book belongs to me.
I have (or I've got) a new car.

— measurement, eg:

▶ contain, cost, hold, measure, weigh

This bottle holds three litres.
How much do you weigh?

— appearance, eg:

▶ appear, look like, matter, seem

You look like a scarecrow.
It doesn't matter.

9.2 Past simple: *I talked*

The past simple is formed as follows: ▶

	I/We You/They He/She/It	talked. didn't talk.
Did	I/we/you/they he/she/it	talk?

Meaning: ▶

Time:	before now
Attitude:	we see a completed act, one which began and ended before now.

Use the past simple
— to make statements about the past: ▶ The lights went out. Someone screamed.
The war lasted thirty years.

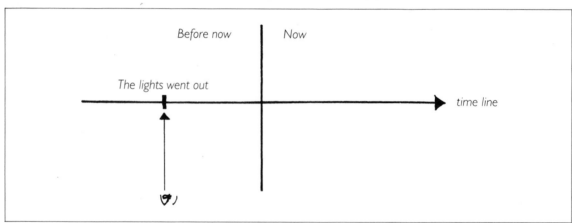

— to tell a story: ▶ One morning, I got up early and went out for a walk. I met an old man with a beard. When I said good morning to him, he ran away...

— with verbs like those in 9.1
(describing measurement, possession,
mental states, appearance, etc: ▶ When I was young, I had a pet dog. Everyone said it looked like a cat. It weighed 12 kilos and lived on fish and chips...

9.3 *used to*

The pattern | *used to* + verb | :

▶ I used to have a dog.
He used to be a heavy smoker.
I used to go to Japan every year.

Used to is like the past form of the present simple, and describes regular past habits (Note that there is no present form of *used to*):

▶

Present:	I do it
Past :	I used to do it

But when you state a definite time, use the past simple:

▶ *Past + time* : I lived there for 10 years

9.4 Continuous forms

The continuous forms have the pattern

| part of *be* + present participle | , *eg:*

▶

Present	am is are	
Past	was were	doing
Perfect	has been	
Future	will be	

Meaning:

▶

Time:	shown by *is/was/will be*, etc
Attitude:	we see an unfinished action, one which started before and goes on after the moment of speaking.

It's raining.
We were just leaving when he arrived.
I've been waiting ages for you.

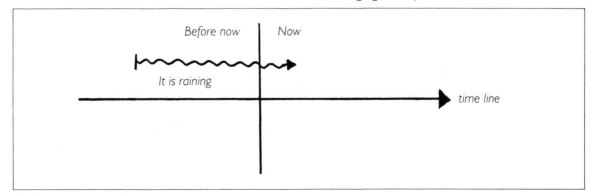

9.5 **Present continuous:** *am/is/are doing*

Meaning:

Time:	now, the moment of speaking, this week, etc
Attitude:	we see an unfinished action, an action in progress.

Use the present continuous for things which are

— happening at this moment:

▶ What are you doing?
I'm making a dress for my sister.

— happening in this period of time:

▶ What is Philip doing nowadays?
He's still studying to be a teacher.
We're not working this week: we're on holiday.
All my friends are trying to give up smoking.

— planned to happen soon:

▶ I'm getting a new car tomorrow.
I'm going to Paris at the weekend.
I'm having dinner with Nick and his girl friend on Friday.

I'm going to Paris at the weekend.

— only temporary:

▶ Michael is usually very sensible, but at the moment he is being very stupid.

Michael is usually very sensible,

but at the moment he is being very stupid.

Have, in the sense of *possess*
is used only in the simple form.
In many expressions, it does not mean
possess, and is used in both simple and
continuous forms:

▶ have breakfast/dinner/lunch; have a bath/a chat/a rest/a shave/a shower/a sleep/a wash/a word.
What time do you usually have breakfast:
We're having dinner in town tonight.
I'll have a word with Joe about the job.
He's not here. He's having a rest.

9.6 Past continuous: *was/were doing*

Meaning:

Time:	before now, earlier than now
Attitude:	we see an unfinished action, one which started before and was still in progress at the time of speaking.

Use the past continuous to describe
background actions in a story:

▶ The Royal Carriage came round the corner. Everywhere, people were waving and cheering. Suddenly, a young man ran out into the street. He was carrying a placard with the words 'Long Live Napoleon' on it. While he was standing there, a policeman came up and arrested him . . .

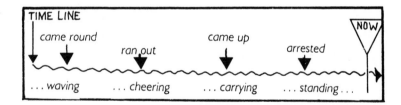

TIME LINE

came round   came up   NOW
        ran out   arrested
. . . waving   . . . cheering   . . . carrying   . . . standing . . .

9.7 Other continuous forms

Use them whenever you are describing
an unfinished action. Start with the
present to see whether you need to
use the continuous form:

▶ (*I'm studying now, and*) I shall still be studying a year from now.
(*I'm waiting here now, and*) I've been waiting here since six o'clock.
He said that he had been waiting there since six o'clock.

10 Perfect tenses

10.1 Form

Form the perfect tenses with

| part of *have* + past participle | eg: ▶

has have had	talked listened been talking been listening

10.2 Present perfect: *has/have talked*

Meaning: ▶

Time:	between 'before now' and 'now'. The exact time is not given.
Attitude:	we are interested in the result of the action, not the time when it happened.

Examples: ▶ Action: Someone has stolen my bicycle.

Someone has stolen my bicycle.

Result: No bicycle!
Action: She has finished the report.
Result: Completed report.

Use the present perfect to describe
— a past action which has present
   results: ▶ Action: John has borrowed my car.
Result: I must go by bus.
Action: We have had a lot of snow.

We have had a lot of snow.

Result: The garden is covered with snow.

The exact time is not specified.

Common time expressions used with the present perfect are:

► just, already, ever, recently, lately, in the last few days, this week

For example:

► Is Kate in?
No, she's just gone out.
Do your homework!
I've already done it!

— something that happened before now, time not specified:

► Have you ever been to Paris?
He's been working very hard.
We haven't seen much of her lately.

Note also the patterns
since + a point of time:
for + a point of time:

► It hasn't rained since May.
► I've been waiting for hours.

When you specify an exact point of time, use the simple past:

► We didn't see her at the party last night.
I waited for hours the other night but nobody came to see me.

You can see the difference in these dialogues:

► Have you ever been to Paris?
Yes, I was there two weeks ago.

► I've lost my pen.
No, you haven't. You lent it to John – I saw you give it to him yesterday.

10.3 Present perfect continuous: *has/have been talking*

Use the continuous form to describe
— something which began before now and is still going on:

► How long has your car been making that strange noise?
I've been trying to open this box for the last forty minutes.

— an activity which finished recently but with results that you notice:

► It's been snowing: the garden is covered with snow.
Have you been smoking? I can smell tobacco on your clothes.
What on earth have you been doing?

What on earth have you been doing?

10.4 Past perfect: *had talked*

Use the past perfect
— to describe an action that happened
earlier in the past than another:

▶ I gave her the present that I had bought the day before.
He had finished his report, and was feeling rather tired,
so he went to bed.

— in reported speech to replace *has/
have . . .ed:*

▶ 'I've broken my arm.'
He told them that he had broken his arm.

— in Type III conditionals:

▶ If he hadn't told us, we wouldn't have known.

'I've broken my arm.'

He told them that he had broken his arm.

If he hadn't told us, we wouldn't have known.

10.5 Past perfect continuous: *had been talking*

Use this form to describe an activity that
was going on in the past before
another:

▶ I had been working all day and was feeling rather tired, so
I went to bed.

I I The Future

I I.I Ways of expressing the future

What we say about the future is usually based on something in the present:

You watch your friend, and you say: ▶ If you drop that plate, it will break.

If you drop that plate, it will break.

You look at the black clouds in the sky, and you say: ▶ It's going to rain.

You have decided to do something and you say: ▶ I'm going to leave school and get a job.

Your sister has written to say that she intends to visit you. You say: ▶ Sarah's coming here for the weekend.

You check the calendar and you say: ▶ Term starts next Monday.

You must choose the form — *will break, going to rain, is coming, starts*, etc — which expresses your attitude to the future event.

I I.2 *will*

Form: ▶

I/We	will	do it.
You/They	'll	be doing it.
He/She/It	won't	have done it.

Use *will*
— to make a simple statement without any special attitude:

▶ You will feel better after you've eaten.
Prices will start to rise again later in the year.
Goodbye. I'll see you later.

— in Type I conditionals:

▶ If you drop that plate, it will break.
You won't grow if you don't eat.

— with *be doing*:

▶ What will you be doing this time next year?

— with *have done*:

▶ They will have eaten by the time we get there.

will also expresses other ideas, such as

— (un)willingness:

▶ My car won't start.
Don't worry, John'll fix it for you.
Mary won't do her homework.

Mary won't do her homework.

— requesting:

▶ Will you pass me the butter, please?

— inviting:

▶ Will you come to the cinema with me?

Sometimes *shall/shan't* is used with *I/we* to express a simple future

— in questions:

▶ Shall we meet you at 7 o'clock or 8 o'clock?
When shall we see you again?

— as a question tag after *Let's*:

▶ Let's have a picnic, shall we?

shall also expresses other ideas, such as

— offering (with *I/we*):

▶ Shall I do that for you?

11.3 *going to*

Form:

▶

I	am	
He/She/It	is	going to do it.
We/You/They	are	

Use *going to*

— to make a statement about the future based on present facts:

present facts	*future result*	*'going to' statement*
black clouds	rain	It's going to rain.
riding carelessly eating too much	accident fat	You're going to fall! She's going to get fat.

— to express a future action based on a present intention:

▶ I'm going to buy you a pet for your birthday.

— with *was/were* in reported speech:

▶ 'I'm going to give it up'.
He told them that he was going to give it up.

11.4 Present tenses to express future

Use the present simple for a regular
planned (timetabled) events:

▶ I have a physics lesson tomorrow.
The plane arrives at 15.30.

The plane arrives at 15.30.

Use the present continuous for an
event which is planned but not
regular or timetabled:

▶ Sarah's coming for the weekend.
When are you leaving for America?

11.5 Summary

Choose the form which expresses
your point of view. For example:
stating a fact, no point of view:

▶ It will rain later.

(or, quoting a calendar):

▶ It's St George's Day tomorrow.

making a personal prediction:

▶ It's going to rain.

stating a planned event:

▶ They're getting married soon.

(or, emphasising their intention):

▶ They're going to get married soon.

11.6 Note on tense used in time clauses

The verb in time clauses is in the
present or present perfect tense, even
though they have a future meaning:

main clause	time clause		
He will meet us	when	he visits London.	(not ~~will visit~~)
Wait here	until	I get back.	(not ~~will get~~)
You can go	as soon as	you have finished.	(not ~~will have~~)

The same is true of Type I conditional
sentences:

We'll go out	even if	it rains tomorrow.	(not ~~will rain~~)
I'll wear my coat	if	I can find it.	(not ~~will be able to~~)
Leave the door open	in case	they've forgotten the key.	(not ~~will have~~)

12 Modals

12.1 Meaning

These are: ▶ may/might can/could/be able to must/have to/have got to/should/ought to, need, dare

All verbs describe actions or states:
You can add modals to verbs to express such ideas as

▶ we talk, you think, he is sleeping

— what is possible or not, eg: ▶ I can swim.
They couldn't go out

— what is permitted or not, eg: ▶ You may go.
You mustn't do that

— probable (likely) or not, eg: ▶ He may be sleeping.
It could be true

This is a hedgehog.

This could be a hedgehog.

12.2 Form

Modals do not change, that is, the form is the same for all persons, eg: ▶

person	modal	main verb
I/We He/She/It You/They	can must should might	talk. be talking. have talked.

You may wait here for me.
John must be working.
She could have come with us.
Do you think this model will work?
It might.

For questions: ▶

person + modal	→	modal + person
They can	→	Can they . . . ?
She could have	→	Could she have . . . ?
You ought to	→	Ought you to . . . ?

Ought you to be out so late?
May I have a look at that?

For negatives: ▶

modal + verb	→	modal + not + verb
must go	→	must not go
could have gone	→	could not have gone

You shouldn't get angry.
I might not be able to see you.

Use short forms in negative questions: ▶ Can't Ann do that for you?

12.3 *may/might*

Use *may*
— to say that you are not certain that something will happen:

▶   I may call round later.
She may be in her office; she may not have left yet.

When you are even less sure, use *might*:

▶   I might call round later, but I doubt it.
She might still be in her office, but she usually leaves before six.

She might still be in her office, but she usually leaves before six.

— to ask permission or to ask politely for something: ▶

May		Yes, you may.
	we go now?	
Can		can.
	I have some tea?	
Could		No, you can't.

Note:
Can't is always used to say 'no'.

12.4 can/could/be able to

Use *can*
— to say that someone knows or does not know how to do something:

▶   Renata can speak several languages.
I can't do this exercise.

— to say that something is possible or impossible:

▶   Onions can make you cry.
I cannot eat another thing!

Use *could*
— as the past tense of *can*:

▶   She could swim like a fish when she was younger.

— as a conditional:

▶   I couldn't eat another thing.
If you had a car, you could give me a lift.

I couldn't eat another thing.

Use *can't* or *cannot* (as the opposite of *must*) to say that something is not logical:

▶ It's time to get up.
It can't be! It's still dark outside.
Somebody called round while you were out. I think it was your brother.
It can't have been my brother: he's still in America.

Use *can/could* to ask for something politely (*could* is more polite):

▶ Hey, Joe, can you lend me ten dollars?
Excuse me, could you tell me how to get to Regent Street, please?

Excuse me, could you tell me how to get to Regent Street, please?

For other tenses, or with other modals,

use part of | *be + able to* | eg: ▶

to be	
will be	
have been	able to
might be	
must have been	

I'd like to be able to speak Greek.
Will you be able to come tonight?
I've never been able to understand mathematics.

Use *can/could* rather than the present and past forms (*am/is/are able to* and *was/were able to*). There is very little difference in meaning between these pairs of sentences:

▶ Can you tell me what happened?
Are you able to tell me what happened?

I couldn't answer his questions.
I wasn't able to answer his questions.

12.5 *must/have to/have got to*

— to express obligation to do or not to do something:

▶ You must come straight home: you mustn't stop to talk to anyone.

Use *must*
— as the opposite of *can't* to say that something is logical:

▶ You must be tired after your journey.
It must have taken you ages to get here.

You must be tired after your journey.

Use *don't have to* (or *don't need to*) to say that there is no obligation:

▶ You don't have to stay if you don't want to.

For other tenses, or with other modals, use part of | *have + to,* | eg:

▶ to have to
having to
will have to
would have to
might have to

I never like having to say goodbye.
You'll have to get up early if you want to see the sunrise.

Use *had to/didn't have to* for the past:

▶ I couldn't come to school yesterday because I had to go to hospital.
She had to attend the meeting but she didn't have to say anything.

Use *must* rather than the present form (*has/have to*). There is very little difference in meaning between this pair of sentences:

▶ We must be home by seven.
We have to be home by seven.

Note, however, the common spoken form *has/have got to:*

▶ We've got to be home by seven.
Have I really got to eat all these peas?

12.6 *should/ought to*

Use *should* to say
— that you expect something to happen as planned:

▶ It's 3 pm. The children usually get home by 3.15 pm. The children should be home soon.

The children should be home soon.

Use *should have* to say
— that you are surprised that something has not happened as planned:

▶ It's 4.15 pm. The children are still not back. The children should have been home an hour ago.

The children should have been home an hour ago.

— to say that it is better to do (or not to do) something:

▶ You should help old people. You shouldn't smoke.

Note
must(n't) means: *Do it! Don't do it!*

should(n't) means: *It is a good thing to do it. It is better not to do it.*

You can use *ought(n't) to* instead of *should(n't)*:

▶ The children ought to be home soon. You oughtn't to smoke so much.

It often suggests that people have not done their duty:

▶ You really ought to write to your parents: they are probably very worried about you.

12.7 need

Need is a regular verb, that is, it adds -*s* in the present with *he/she/it* and uses *do/does/did* in questions and negative statements:

▶ He needs a haircut.

He needs a haircut.

You don't need to come if you don't want to.
Do you need to change any money?
We didn't need to change trains.

There is a modal form, but it is now only used in the negative:

▶ needn't   needn't have

You needn't come if you don't want to.
You needn't have changed any money.

There is a difference in meaning between *needn't have* and *didn't need to*.

Needn't have can only mean you did something which was not necessary:

▶ I needn't have taken an umbrella.
can only mean
I took an umbrella because I thought it was going to rain. In fact it didn't rain, so the umbrella was unnecessary.

Didn't need to means that an action was not necessary (whether you did it or not):

▶ I didn't need to take an umbrella.
may mean
I didn't take an umbrella because I knew that it was not going to rain.
or
I took an umbrella because I thought it was going to rain. In fact it didn't rain, so the umbrella was unnecessary.

12.8 *dare*

Dare has a modal form, which is used only in the present:

▶ Is your father really a spy?
I daren't tell you.
How dare you talk to me like that?

In the past, *dare* is regular:

▶ Maria didn't dare to go into the house by herself.

13 Conditionals

13.1 Meaning

Conditionals show how one situation,
the condition, produces another,
the consequence:

the condition	the consequence
If John has time, If I lived nearer, If he had taken the train.	he will call round to see you. I could visit you more often. he would have arrived earlier.

If you take the train, you'll get there quicker.

If you took the train, you'd save time.

If you'd taken the train, you'd have arrived by now.

There are three main types of condition:

I   the world as it is:
If you take the train, you'll get there quicker. (= There is a real chance that you will take the train.)
II   the world as it might be, not as it is:
If you took the train, you'd save time. (= It is less likely that you will take the train.)
III   the world as it might have been:
If you'd taken the train, you'd have arrived by now. (= But of course you didn't take the train.)

13.2 Form

| Type I | | |
If present (do, is doing, has done)	,	will or imperative or modal
If you have time	,	will you come round?
If you are not doing anything later	,	come and see us.
If you have finished your homework	,	you might be able to help us.
Type II		
If past (did)	,	**would or modal**
If I had time,	,	I would go to night school.
If you went to Hollywood	,	you could become a filmstar
Type III		
If past perfect (had done)	,	**would have or modal**
If you hadn't been so lazy	,	you would have been in time for breakfast.
If he had come earlier	,	he might have been able to help us.

You can put the conditional clause second (leave out the comma):

▶ Come and see us if you have time.
I could go to America if I wanted to.
He could have helped us if he'd come earlier.

When *if* means every time, the sentence pattern is

| *if* + present , present |:

▶ If you drop eggs, they break.

If you drop eggs, they break.

In Type II conditionals, use the special form *If I were* to refer to an impossible condition:

If I were you, I'd get married today.

14 The passive

14.1 Meaning

The subject of any sentence is what is the most important thing in our minds as we speak. Here are two sentences. The first is about my grandfather; the second is about a bomb:

subject	verb	object
My grandfather	built	this house in 1888.
The bomb	injured	several people.

The passive form is used when the object is the most important thing in our minds. Now, the first sentence is about a house; the second sentence is about some injured people:

▶

subject	verb
This house	was built in 1888.
Several people	were injured.

If it is important to you, you can still mention the agent (my grandfather, the bomb) using *by*:

▶

subject	verb	agent
It	was built in 1888	by my grandfather.
They	were injured	by a bomb.

Notice that the information is the same. It is our attitude (point of view) which is different.

Another example:
We have a dog called Brandy. He is my daughter Sarah's dog, and she usually feeds him – but sometimes she forgets. When I come home at night, I ask one of two questions:

If I want to know if Sarah has been a good girl, I ask:
I am thinking about Sarah.

▶ Has Sarah fed Brandy yet?

If I am worried about the dog, I ask:
I am thinking about Brandy.

▶ Has Brandy been fed yet?

14.2 Form

Form the passive with part of

| *be* + past participle, | : |

▶

to be	
being	
am/is/are	
was/were	moved
will be	done
would be	
have been	
can be	

Something	has to be	done.	
John	is being	examined	by a doctor.
Gorillas	are	found	in Africa.
The gun	was	taken	from him.
The meeting	will be	held	in London.
Millions	have been	spent	on new roads.
I	can be	reached	on 235–1212.

When a verb has both a direct and an indirect object, either can become the subject of a verb in the passive:

▶ We gave   the boys   a map.

The direct object (a map) can become the subject:

▶ A map   was given   to the boys.

The indirect object (the boys) can become the subject:

▶ The boys   were given   a map.

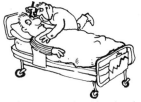

John is being examined by the doctor.

Other examples where the indirect object becomes the subject of the verb in the passive:

▶ We have told them the truth →
They have been told the truth.

They taught us Latin at school →
We were taught Latin at school.

They will ask you a lot of questions →
You will be asked a lot of questions.

Did anyone show her the Crown Jewels? →
Was she shown the Crown Jewels?

14.3 Common uses of the passive

The passive is often used
— in public notices with the part of
  be left out:

▶ | ENGLISH SPOKEN HERE |

| NO CHANGE GIVEN |

| CHILDREN UNDER 14 NOT ADMITTED |

| BOOKS BOUGHT AND SOLD |

— in scientific writing:

▶ The idea was first developed in the sixties. The first serious experiments were carried out in California in 1973. The first model was built in 1975. By 1982, over one million had been sold.

— whenever the agent (see 14.1) is
  not important:

▶ It is said (= They say) that by the year 2000, the world's rain forests will have been destroyed (= men will have destroyed them).

15 The imperative:

15.1 Meaning

The imperative tells someone to do something:

▶ Go away!
Don't bother me!

or, using *let us* (*let's*), makes a suggestion:

▶ Let's go.
Let's not wait any longer.

15.2 Form

The base form of the verb without *you*: ▶
The negative is always formed with

$\boxed{don't + \text{base form}}$:

Stop! Look! Listen to me!

▶ Don't talk nonsense!
Don't be silly!

Note that imperatives are often followed by an exclamation mark.

15.3 Uses

Use the imperative
— to give directions:

▶ Turn left, then right, then go straight on.

— to give an order:

▶ Be quiet!

— to give instructions:

▶ Empty the contents into a cup, add boiling water and stir well.

— to warn:

▶ Look out!
Don't touch that switch!
Mind your head!

— to invite:
(often with *please*)

▶ Come in! Sit down!
Please sit down!
Please don't wait for me.

— on public notices:

▶ | Cross now |

| Keep left |

| Mind the step |

| Do not talk to the driver |

| Do not cross the line |

— in written instructions:

▶ Put the beans in a dish, pour on cold water and leave for twenty minutes.

15.4 Uses of *let*

There are two patterns with *let*. The first is

$\boxed{\textit{Let's (not)} + \text{verb}}$. Use this pattern to make suggestions:

▶ Let's see who can finish first.
Let's not argue.

The second is

$\boxed{\textit{(Don't) let} + \text{object} + \text{verb}}$. In this pattern, *let* means *allow*:

▶ Let him speak.
Don't let them get away.

15.5 Polite imperatives

The tone of voice is very important. You can make imperatives more polite by adding *please* before or after the imperative:

▶ Shut the door, please.
Please don't shout!

Shut the door!

To be even more polite, use expressions like *Could you . . . ?* or *Would you mind . . . ?*:

▶ Could you shut the door, please?
Would you mind not shouting?

Could you shut the door, please?

16 Gerund and infinitive

16.1 Gerund

Add *-ing* to any verb to make a kind of verbal noun called a gerund:
The gerund can be the subject or the object of a verb:

▶ talk → talking, mean → meaning

▶ Swimming is a good form of exercise.
I enjoy swimming.

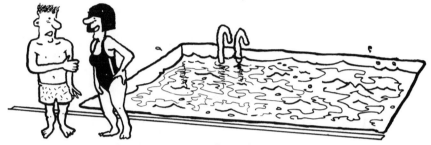

Swimming is a good form of exercise.

Like a verb, it can take an object:

▶ Smoking cigarettes is bad for you.
You should stop smoking cigarettes.

Always use the gerund form of the verb
— after prepositions:

▶
He succeeded	in	passing his driving test.
I'm thinking	of	going to Portugal.
She is used	to	working long hours.
You cannot live	without	making mistakes.
I'm no good	at	telling jokes.

— after these verbs:

▶ avoid, dislike, enjoy, finish, give up, go on, can't help, keep (on), mind, practise

Try to	avoid	losing your temper.
I	dislike	having to get up early.
Do you	enjoy	being a teacher?
Has he	finished	painting the house yet?
He has	given up	going to committee meetings.
We can't	go on	meeting like this.
I can't	help	laughing.
Why does he	keep (on)	smiling at me?
Would you	mind	closing the door?
You should	practise	saying 'Six Swiss wrist watches'.

— in the common expressions:

▶ It's no good/no use/not worth + -ing

It's no good asking me about algebra — I never did maths at school.
It's no use crying over spilt milk. (proverb)
It's not worth going out now — all the shops are closed.

16.2 Infinitive

Use the base infinitive (ie, base form
of the verb)
— after modals:

▶ You must wait.
It might be true.
He shouldn't do that.

— after *let* and *make*:

▶ They won't let me watch television.
Don't make me laugh.

They won't let me watch television.

— in the pattern

| *see/feel/hear/smell/watch*
+ object + infinitive, | eg:

▶

	see, etc	object	infinitive
I	saw	Smith	win the race.
You	could hear	a pin	drop.
Joe	felt	someone	touch his arm.

(For the difference between, eg,
watch him do it and *watch him doing it*,
see 17.1).

Use the *to*-infinitive
— to express intention:

▶ He pushed the car to make it start.
I've come to see if you need anything.
He stopped to light a cigarette.

He pushed the car to make it start.

— after these verbs:

▶ afford, agree, arrange, bother, decide, deserve, expect, fail, hesitate, hope, intend, learn, long, manage, mean, pretend, promise, refuse, try, want, wish

He has agreed to help us.
She didn't even bother to telephone.
I've decided to become a nun.
When did you learn to speak Arabic?
We've managed to save a thousand pounds.
Please try to be on time in future!

— in the pattern

| *teach/etc + him + to do something* |

:

▶ My father taught me not to tell lies.

Other verbs like *teach* are:

▶ allow, ask, expect, get, help, invite, permit, tell, want

He	asked	me	to explain everything.
Mum	expects	us	to be home by six.
I'll	get	him	to give you a hand.
She	told	them	to be quiet.
I	want	you	to listen carefully.

16.3 Verb + gerund or infinitive

Some verbs may be followed by the gerund or the *to*-infinitive:

▶ stop, try, forget, remember;
hate, like, love, prefer;
begin, start

The two patterns have different meanings

— *stop*:

▶ Why have you stopped working? =
You should be working, and you are not working.
I've stopped to have a drink. =
I've stopped because I want a drink.

I've stopped to have a drink.

— *try*:

▶ Problem : I am overweight.
Objective: I must try to lose weight.
Method : I'll try eating less.

remember and *forget*

Use these words to talk about a past event.
To say that your memory was or wasn't
working **at the time of the event**. Use

| past + *to*-infinitive | :

▶

past	**to-infinitive**
I remembered	to get a loaf.

I remembered to get a loaf.

Did you remember	to say goodbye to Joe?
I forgot	to pay for the loaf.
She didn't forget	to send me a postcard.

I forgot to pay for the loaf.

To say that your memory of the past
event is or isn't working **now** use

| present + gerund | :

▶

present	**gerund**
I remember	going into the shop.

I remember going into the shop.

(The pattern *I forget doing* is not very
common).

hate, like, love, prefer
Use the *to*-infinitive after the forms
would like to, would love to.
would hate to, would prefer to:

| but | |
| I don't remember | seeing Mary there. |

▶ Would you like to come with us?
I'd love to come with you.
I'd hate to be in your shoes when your father finds out!

In other cases, there is very little difference of meaning between the gerund and the infinitive:
Use the gerund to talk about regular, general habits:
Use the infinitive if you are thinking about a particular time:

▶ I like wearing old clothes, but I hate having to wear suits.

▶ I like to dress up if I am going to a party.
I hate to bother you, but could you help me for a moment?

begin, start
You can use either the gerund or the infinitive: there is very little difference of meaning:

▶ I began studying music when I was five.
He began to cry when he heard the news.
When did you first start wearing long trousers?
She started to back away when the dog came into the room.

17 Participles

17.1 The present participle: *talking*

It has the same form as the gerund,

ie, | base + *ing* | :

▶ talk → talking, go → going

Use the present participle:
— after a part of *be* to form the continuous tenses:

▶ I'm going out.
He's been working in the garden.
It must have been raining.

He's been working in the garden.

— after *go* to describe many sports and other activities, eg:

▶ go bowling, go dancing, go fishing, go hiking, go sailing, go shopping, go skiing, go swimming

It was such a lovely day that we decided to go swimming.
We went skiing in Austria last year.
Where's Mike? He's gone fishing.

— in the pattern | *see him doing* | :
Other verbs used in this pattern are:

▶ I saw him getting into his car.
▶ feel, hear, smell, watch

I can hear a baby crying.
I like to watch the children playing in the park.

There is a difference between *saw him doing* and *saw him do*.

He was getting into his car.

saw him doing describes the action in progress:
saw him do describes the whole action from start to finish:

▶ I saw him getting into his car

▶ I saw him get into his car and drive off.

I saw him getting into his car.

I saw him get into his car and drive off.

Other examples:

I could hear the rain falling on the roof.
I heard something hit the window. A small bird had flown into it.
Can you smell something burning?
We decided to stay on the beach to watch the sun go down.

— in the pattern ╎ *needs doing* ╎. The expression *needs doing* means the same as *needs to be done*:

▶ Your hair needs cutting. =
Your hair needs to be cut.

17.2 The past participle: *talked*

To form the past participle add *-(e)d* to the base form:
(For irregular forms, like *go – gone, speak – spoken*, see 8.4.)

▶ talk → talked, move → moved

Use the past participle
— to form the perfect tenses:

▶ Have you talked to your lawyer yet?
He said he had never been to Austria.
You should have waited until the others had finished.

— in the pattern ╎ *have something done* ╎.

It means something must be done, and I will ask someone else to do it for me:

▶ I must repair the car. =
I will do it myself.

I must repair the car.

I must have the car repaired. =
I will pay someone else to do it.

I must have the car repaired.

83

Other examples:

► Where do you have your hair done?
John has just had his house painted.

You can use *get* instead of *have*:

► I must get the car repaired.
When are you going to get your hair cut?

Get suggests extra effort or difficulty, and it may be a thing you will have to do yourself:

► This room is a mess: I really must get it tidied up.
Try to get your homework done before your mother comes home.

Participles are often used as adjectives:
— present participle:

► an interesting book, an exciting story, a terrifying experience

— past participle:

► a stolen car, a frozen lake, a well-known landmark

18 Phrasal verbs

18.1 Meaning

A phrasal verb is a compound verb formed by a verb and a particle. The combinations are:
— verb + adverb, eg: ▶ get away, fall out
— verb + preposition, eg: ▶ look for, take after
— verb + adverb + preposition, eg: ▶ run out of, put up with

A phrasal verb is like a chemical compound:

Sodium [Na] + Chlorine [Cl] → [NaCl] = common salt				
give	+ up	→	give up	= surrender
take	+ after	→	take after	= resemble

Sometimes the meaning of the phrasal verb is not very different from the meaning of the parts:

▶ Please sit down!
The Smiths have gone away on holiday.
You'll have to do without milk today.
Go on with your work.
Drop in and see us when you are next in London.

In other cases, you cannot guess the meaning from the parts, but only from the situation:

▶ I have nowhere to stay. Can you put me up for a few nights? (= accommodate me)
I came across it when I was in Crete. (= I found it)
Snobs look down on ordinary people.

Notice that a phrasal verb may have more than one meaning. For example: ▶ take off = remove
Take your clothes off.
take off = depart
The plane takes off at 12.30.
take off = be successful
Do you think this book will take off?
take off = imitate, mimic
She's a wonderful mimic. She can take anyone off.

Take your clothes off.

The plane takes off at 12.30.

Do you think this book will take off?

FLO JONES AS MAGGIE THATCHER

She's a wonderful mimic. She can take anyone off.

18.2 Form

Common verbs used in phrasals are
▶ be, break, bring, call, carry, come, cut, draw, drop, fall, get, give, go, hand, hold, keep, let, look, make, put, run, set, take, turn

The particles used in phrasals may be
— adverbs:
▶ away, back, forward, out

— prepositions:
▶ after, against, at, for, from, into, like, to, with, without

— either adverbs or prepositions:
▶ about, across, along, around, before, behind, by, down, in, off, on, over, round, through, under, up

Examples with adverb particles:
▶ The meeting has been put off until Monday. (= postponed).
Is that true or did you make it up? (= invent).
Carry on writing until I tell you to stop. (= continue).
We couldn't believe that he was really a thief. We were completely taken in by his smart appearance. (= deceived).

Examples with preposition particles:
▶ Will you look after the house while I'm away? (= take care of).
Janet has really fallen for Joe. (= become attracted to him).

Examples of particles which may be either adverb or preposition:
▶ They didn't like my plan so they turned it down. (= rejected it).
The lorry came to Leys Avenue and turned down it. (= entered it).

The position of the object of a phrasal verb depends on whether the particle is an adverb or a preposition.

When the particle is an adverb and the object is a personal pronoun, you must use the pattern VOP:
▶

verb	object	particle
take	it	off
bring	them	back
let	me	down

When the particle is a preposition, you must use the pattern VPO in all cases: ▶

verb	particle	object
take	after	your father
take	after	him

*He takes after his father.

With verb + adverb phrasals, when the object is not a personal pronoun, you may use either pattern: ▶

VOP: Take your coat off.
VPO: Take off your coat.

The VOP pattern is preferred when the object is
— one of the pronouns *somebody, nothing, everyone, anything,* etc: ▶

Take everything off.
Put somebody up.
Give nothing away.

— a short noun phrase: ▶

Put your books away.
Take your coat off.

The pattern VPO is preferred
— when the object is a long noun phrase: ▶

Switch off all the lights in the house.
He made up a very amusing story about a dishonest lawyer and a blind chicken.
I'll put on the blue dress with the white collar.

— for the sake of rhythm: ▶

give up smoking, take up surfing

* from *Making Sense of Phrasal Verbs* by Martin Shovel, Cassell 1985

18.3 The use of phrasal verbs

Phrasal verbs are common in speaking and in informal writing, and are often preferred to a single longer word with nearly the same meaning:

▶ She made it up   *for*   She invented it.
Please go on   *for*   Please continue.
Put it out   *for*   Extinguish it.

I propose to continue to endeavour to discover the reason why women will never reveal their age.

means, more simply:

▶ I shall go on trying to find out why women will never let on how old they are.

I shall go on trying to find out why women will never let on how old they are.

You can hear new phrasal verbs every day especially among young people:

▶ This music turns me on = It excites me.
Don't put me down = Don't humiliate me.

Like slang, most of these expressions don't last, so you should be careful about using them.

19 Adverbials

19.1 Meaning

Verbs describe actions or states:
Adverbials say something more about the action or state, such as how, where or when it happened:

▶ speak, go, love

▶ speak loudly, go today, love forever

Speak loudly

They also modify the meaning of adjectives and other adverbs:

▶ It's good. It's very good, but it isn't good enough.
He speaks quickly. He speaks too quickly.

19.2 Form

An adverbial can be
— a single word (an adverb):

— a phrase:

— a clause:

▶ loudly, there, soon, sometimes, still

▶ by chance, one afternoon, all the time, as a matter of fact

▶ whenever I see her, as soon as I can

Add *-ly* to adjectives to form adverbs which answer the question *how?*:

▶

adjective	adverb
bad	badly
polite	politely
useful	usefully
happy	happily
terrible	terribly

A bad driver drives badly.
A polite man answers politely.

To make comparisons, use *more +* adverb:

▶ He drives more carefully than I do.

Special cases:

▶

adjective	adverb	comparative
good	well	better
hard	hard	harder
fast	fast	faster
bad	badly	worse

He's a good driver: he drives well.
He drives better than I do.
She works very hard; harder than anyone else in the office.

19.3 Word order

Adverbials go at the beginning, in the middle, or at the end of a sentence:

Position I	Subject	Aux/ modal	Position II	Main verb	Object complement	Position III
Carefully,	John			opened	the box.	
Every week,	she			visits	her parents.	
Frankly,	I	do not		like	his wife.	
	John		**carefully**	opened	the box.	
	People		**often**	say	silly things.	
	He	did not	**even**	say	goodbye.	
	I	have	**just**	seen	him.	
	The boys		**always**	used to enjoy	themselves.	
	We		**hardly ever**	did	any homework.	
	You		**really**	ought to be	more careful.	
	John			opened	the box	**very carefully.**
	She			plays	the piano	**very well.**
	There			is	a funny smell	**in here.**
	He	did not		do	it	**on purpose.**

Notice that adverbials
— come immediately after *am/is/are/was/were:*   ▶

subject	be	adverb	complement
I	am	really	nervous.
John	is	never	nice.
We	are	just	good friends.
She	was	once	a policewoman.
They	were	still	in bed.

— come immediately after the subject in short answers: ▶

Who does the washing-up, you or Susan?
I usually do.

Robert's in a bad mood this morning.
He often is.

— are not put between a verb and its object: ▶

She usually does her work very well.
(not ~~does usually her work~~ or ~~does very well her work~~)

When an adverbial can be put in more than one place in a sentence, there is a slight change of meaning. We usually put an adverbial at the beginning (Position I) so as to focus attention on it.

Without focus:

▶ John carefully opened the door.

With focus:

▶ Carefully, John opened the door.

Similarly, the adverbial at the end (Position III) is the focus of attention.

Focus on the time (ten):

▶ I'll see you on Friday at ten.

Focus on the day (Friday):

▶ I'll see you at ten on Friday.

19.4 Adverbials of place

These adverbials answer the question *where?* or *where to?*:

▶ Where is it?   Over there.
Where are you going? Into the garden.

Many adverbs of place are used in phrasal verbs:

▶ go away, set off, come back

The commonest adverbs of place are *here* and *there*:

▶ here = in *or* to this place
there = in *or* to that place

Bring it here. Here it is!
Put it there.   There it is!

Bring it here. Put it there.

They are often used in the pattern

| preposition + *here/there* | :

▶ Put it over there.
Are there many wild animals round here?
What's that up there?

The patterns *Here it is/Here they are*
and *There it is/There they are* answer
the question *'where?'*:

► Where's my jacket?
Here it is.
Where are my glasses?
There they are – on your head.

There's a . . ./There are . . .
Use the pattern: *There's a   B   in   C:*

► There's a lion in the garden.
(*not* ~~In the garden is a lion.~~)
There's some butter in the fridge, but there aren't
any eggs.

Other common adverbials of place are: ►

indoors, outdoors, upstairs, downstairs, next door,
upside down, inside out, back to back, back to front,
face to face, side by side, up and down, in and out

I live next door to a Waxworks' Museum.

They've hung this painting upside down.

He put his jacket on back to front.

Use adverbs ending in *-wards* only with verbs of movement:

▶ backwards, forwards, inwards, outwards, upwards, downwards, westwards, eastwards, northwards, southwards.

A pendulum swings backwards and forwards.

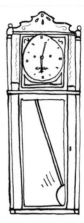

A pendulum swings backwards and forwards.

19.5 Adverbials of time

These adverbials answer the questions
— *When?*

▶ I have to leave soon.
I have to leave early tomorrow morning.
See you on Friday at one o'clock.

— *How long?*

▶ He came for a week and stayed for a month.
I have been here since last Friday.
He spent all morning on the phone.
She spent the whole day writing letters.

— *How often?*

▶ I don't often see my brother.
We see each other three times a week.
The milk is delivered daily (every day).

The order of time adverbials is usually
— from the particular to the general:

▶ day – month – year
On Friday, the second of May, 1988

The time of day may come after the day:

▶ See you on Friday at one o'clock.

— how long, how often, when:

▶

	how long?	how often?	when?
We meet	for an hour	every Friday.	
We met	briefly		last week.
We met		twice	last year.

Common time expressions to
answer the question
— *When?*

earlier	now	later
yesterday yesterday morning last night the day before yesterday last week the week before last two weeks ago	today this morning tonight this week	tomorrow tomorrow morning tomorrow night the day after tomorrow next week the week after next in two weeks' time
How many times? once, twice, three times, four times, etc once a day, twice a week, three times a year, etc every day, every other day, every three weeks, etc hourly, daily, weekly, monthly, yearly		

— *How often?*

▶ never, hardly ever, seldom
   sometimes, occasionally
   often, usually
   always, ever, forever

yet and *still*
Use *(not) . . . yet* in questions and
negative sentences to describe
something that you expect to happen.
yet usually goes at the end of the
sentence:

▶ Has the post arrived yet?
   Aren't you ready yet?
   It hasn't arrived yet.
   Have you finished? Not yet.

Aren't you ready yet?

Use *still* in positive sentences and
questions to describe something that
began in the past and is continuing
into the future:

▶ Do you still live in Howard Road?
My daughter works in a bank, but my son is still at school.

Use *still . . . not* when you are angry,
surprised or worried about something
which you expected to happen:

▶ Kate usually arrives home at 3 pm.
At 3.30 pm you aren't worried, so you say:
Kate isn't back yet.
At 6.00 pm you are worried and you say:
Kate still isn't back!
John promised to mend my bike three weeks ago, and he
still hasn't mended it.

Kate isn't back yet.

Kate still isn't back!

not . . . any longer/not . . . any more
Use *not . . . any longer* or *not . . . any
more* when the action has stopped:

▶ Does Nicola still work here?
No, she doesn't work here any more.
I'm sorry, I can't wait any longer.

19.6 Other adverbials

We also use adverbials
— to describe degree (they answer
the question *how much?*):

▶ extremely, fairly, quite, rather, very, too

We're fairly busy every day, but we're extremely busy
on Saturdays.
It was raining quite hard when we left.
It's rather dark in here.
He is a very good typist. He types very well.
It's too late to go to the cinema now.

It's rather dark in here.

Notice the difference between *too*
and *very*:

▶ This is very heavy. I can only just lift it.
This is too heavy. I can't lift it.

— to list ideas:

▶ First(ly)... Secondly... Next... Then... Finally...
First, put the beans in the pan. Then, cover them with
water.

— to join ideas:

▶ For example... In other words... On the other hand...
Anyway... In any case...
I don't feel like going out tonight. In any case, I haven't got
any money.

— to express viewpoint or attitude:

▶ Frankly, I don't care what you think.
I just don't care.
I don't care at all.

Some adverbials of this kind come at
the beginning of the sentence, eg:

▶ Actually...
As a matter of fact,...
Basically...
Between you and me...
Of course...
Perhaps...
Personally...
Unfortunately...

Some come in mid-position, eg:

▶ almost, also, just, only
I almost died when I heard the news.
He's got two cats. He's also got a dog.
I just don't know what to do next.
You can only do your best.

Some come at the end, eg:

▶ as well = too
Can I come as well?
not... at all
I don't mind at all.

The adverb *else* always comes after the
word it modifies:

▶ Are you still hungry? Would you like anything else?
Gianni knows. Who else knows?
I'll have to stay with my parents. I have nowhere else
to go.

20 Conjunctions

20.1 Meaning

Conjunctions join words, phrases or sentences:

▶ It was late — We went to bed →
It was late so we went to bed.
We went to bed because it was late.

Some conjunctions make a simple link, like the links in a chain:

▶ and, but, either . . . or, neither . . . nor, or, so

bread and butter, heads or tails
neither useful nor attractive
She's either drunk or crazy.
Play in the garden but not on the road.
He got up and left the meeting.
It was late so we went to bed.
Go away or I'll call the police.

Heads or tails?

She's either drunk or crazy.

Others show relationships, such as
— time when:
— reason why:
— place where:

▶ What will you do after you have finished your course?
▶ We're learning English because we have to.
▶ Wherever you go, I'll go too.

20.2 Time

Conjunctions which express time are: ▶ after, as (= when), as long as, as soon as, before, since, until, when, whenever, while

They arrived just as we were leaving.
Did anyone call while I was out?
Stay as long as you like.

They arrived just as we were leaving.

before and *after* may be followed by a clause or a participle: ▶

Please lock up before you leave.
before leaving.

I phoned him after I had read the report.
after reading

Note that the verb in the time clause is in the present or present perfect, even though it refers to the future: ▶

Wait here until I finish.
I'll let you know the results as soon as I know them.

20.3 Place

Conjunctions which express place are: ▶ as far as, where, wherever

We walked as far as we could.
Do you know where Helen has gone to?
I'll follow you wherever you go.

Note the use of *as far as* in these expressions: ▶

As far as I know, he isn't married.
You can go to the devil as far as I'm concerned.

20.4 Other relationships

There are also conjunctions to express
other ideas such as:

— cause: ▶ as, because, since, seeing that

As he was the only one who could speak Portuguese, he
was sent to Brazil.
Seeing that there are only five minutes left, why don't we
have a singsong?

— purpose: ▶ so that

He wanted to earn some money so that he could buy a
car.

— result: ▶ so ... that, such a(n) ... that

It was so cold that the sea froze.
It was such a cold day that the sea froze.
She spoke so softly that I could hardly hear what she said.

It was such a cold day that the sea froze.

— condition: ▶ as long as, if, in case, unless

You can have a party as long as you don't make a mess.
Take some sandwiches in case you get hungry.
Some people won't go out at night unless they have to.

— comparison: ▶ as if, as though

He looked $\begin{cases} \text{as if} \\ \text{as though} \end{cases}$ he had seen a ghost.

He looked as if he had seen a ghost.

— concession:

▶   although, even though, even if

He went to work $\begin{cases} \text{even though} \\ \text{although} \end{cases}$ he was ill.

Ring me when you get home, even if it's late.

20.5 Conjunctions used in reported speech

To report what someone says, use *that:* ▶

'I'm ill'
John says that he is ill.
'I don't eat meat'
Is it true that you don't eat meat?

To report a yes/no question, use *if* or *whether*:

▶   'Are you ill?'
I asked him if he was ill.
'Is there any point in working hard?'
He wondered whether there was any point in working hard.

21 Reported Speech

21.1 Meaning

When A says something to me, I may
want to tell you what A said, ie, I want
to report his words, using such
reporting verbs as:

▶ say, ask, tell

A's words may be a statement or a
question:

	A's words to me	reporting verb	A's reported words
statement	'I'll do it'	A says	(that)* he will do it.
question	'Are you happy?' 'Why did you cry?'	A asked me A wants to know	if I was happy. why I cried.

*You can leave out *that*.

You can also report an imperative:

▶ 'Go!' →
A told me to go.
▶ 'Don't go! →'
A told me not to go.

21.2 Form

If the reporting verb is in the past
tense, the tense of the reported verb
also changes to a past form:

from	to	A's words	reporting verb in past	reported verb to past
move/moves	→ moved	It smells.	A thought that	it smelled.
don't/doesn't	→ didn't	I don't care.	A said that	he didn't care.
moved	→ had moved	You lied!	A said that	I had lied.
am/is	→ was	I'm shy.	A said	he was shy.
are	→ were	Are you shy?	A wondered if	I was shy.
has/have	→ had	Has it gone?	A asked me if	it had gone.
will	→ would	I'll do it.	A said that	he would do it.
can	→ could	You can stay.	A told us that	we could stay.
may	→ might	It may happen.	A thought that	it might happen.
must	→ had to	I must go.	A told us that	he had to go.

Might does not change:

might → might
It might rain.
A thought that it might rain.

Words referring to time and place usually change. For example:

here → there
Is any one here? →
He asked if any one was there.

tomorrow → the next day
I'll go tomorrow →
He said he would go the next day.

yesterday → the day before
We saw them yesterday →
Didn't you say that you had seen them the day before?

ago → before
I met her two years ago →
He said he had met her two years before.

The tense of the reported verb does not change
— when the reporting verb is in the present, present perfect or future:

▶ He loves me → I know that he loves me.
It's OK   → I've heard that it's OK.
He's mad   → They'll tell you he's mad.

— when you are stating a true fact, even if the reporting verb is in the past:

Fact: ▶   The Earth goes round the Sun.
Present: ▶ Everyone knows that the Earth goes round the Sun.
Past: ▶   Our teacher told us that the Earth goes round the Sun.

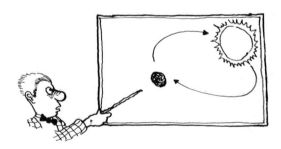

Our teacher told us that the Earth goes round the Sun.

— in the case of modals, when the
situation referred to still exists:

▶ You must go this evening.
What did he say?
He said that we must go this evening.

You should be careful.
They told me that I should be careful.

You should be careful.

They told me that I should be careful.

Note the difference when the
situation no longer exists:

▶ He said that we had to go that evening.
They told me I should have been more careful.

21.3 Reporting verbs

The pattern of reporting verbs is:

subject	reporting verb	person reported to indirect object	words reported direct object
John	told	me	(that) he was ill.

These verbs never have an indirect
object:

▶ answer, believe, deny, doubt, expect, feel, hope, notice,
observe, see, suppose, think, understand

Put in the indirect object with these verbs:

▶ assure, inform, persuade, promise, remind, tell, warn

	reporting verb	indirect object	
He	assured informed persuaded promised reminded told warned	me us everyone me his wife nobody his boss	that he would do it.

These verbs may have an indirect object, always with *to*:

▶ admit, announce, complain, explain, mention, point out, report, say, suggest

For example:
Without indirect object:
With indirect object:

▶ John explained that he wasn't well.
▶ John explained to us that he wasn't well.

21.4 Reporting questions

When a question is reported, the question form and the question mark disappear.
The pattern is:

subject	reporting verb	(indirect object)	question word	reported question		
				subj	verb	complement/object
I	wonder		where	she	keeps	her money.

When there is no question word, ie in yes/no questions, use *if* or *whether*:

I asked him { if / whether } he was happy.

Other examples:

Where are they? →
I'd like to know where they are.

I'd like to know where they are.

How can I help you? →
He asked us how he could help us.
Who do you want? →
They asked him who he wanted.
Who wants you? →
They asked him who wanted him.
Do you like celery? →
The cook wants to know if you like celery.

You can also add the words *or not* at the end of the clause:

▶ He asked me $\begin{cases} \text{if} \\ \text{whether} \end{cases}$ I was ready to come or not.

22 Punctuation

22.1 Summary of punctuation marks

Some separate words or groups of words:

the full stop	.	This is the end.
the comma	,	The army, the navy and the air force.
semi-colon	;	He has many problems: spelling; writing; reading.
colon	:	There's only one word for it: terrible.
brackets	( )	Joe Brown (1890–1962) lived here.

Some show the type of sentence:

the question mark	?	Who are you?
exclamation mark	!	Get out of my house!
inverted commas	' ' or " "	Have you got a book called 'Making Sense of English Idioms', please?

The hyphen joins two or more words to make one word:

► She is a well-known author.

The apostrophe
— shows that a letter is missing:

► haven't, can't, won't

— marks the possessive form of nouns:

► It's a dog's life.

It's a dog's life.

22.2 Marks which separate

Use the full stop [.]
— at the end of a sentence (unless there is a question or exclamation mark):

► I wish I hadn't eaten those beans.

— after a shortened word:

► pron. Dept. Eng. N. Carolina

— in decimal expressions:

► 3.79 (three point seven nine)
.009 (point oh oh nine)

You don't need a full stop
— after shortened titles:

► Mr Mrs Ms Dr

— in commonly-used initials:

► NATO UNESCO EEC USSR USA

Use the comma to separate
— groups of words, such as adverbials, from the main sentence:

Frankly, I think she's too old to be a model.
► I decided, after a lot of thought, to go back to bed.

— the reporting verb from the words actually spoken:

► 'That's the one,' he answered.
'It is time,' she said, 'you gave up.'

— thousands in whole numbers:

► 3,542,609 (three million, five hundred and forty-two thousand, six hundred and nine)

— items in a list (except before *and*):   ▶   I need bread, milk, eggs, margarine and some cheese.

When each item consists of several words, you can use the semi colon instead: ▶   The job has many parts: sorting and filing; typing; word processing; taking shorthand and audio dictation; answering the phone; and helping to show visitors round.

Use the colon
— to introduce a list of items: ▶   The job has many parts: sorting and filing; typing; taking shorthand.

— to 'announce' an answer: ▶   The answer is simple: shoot them all.

Use brackets ( ) to close off extra information: ▶   Neil Armstrong (USA) was the first man on the moon.

22.3 Marks which show the type of sentence

Use the question mark [?] only at the end of direct questions: ▶   Who are you?
Is that your camel?

Do not use the question mark after indirect (reported) questions: ▶   He wants to know who you are.
Everyone wonders if that is your camel.

Use the exclamation mark
— after imperatives: ▶   Go! Don't ask me!
— after words which express strong feelings, eg: ▶   Ugh!   = unpleasant
Wow! = exciting, remarkable
Hm!   = interesting
Hmm! = nice, tasty
Ouch! = That hurts!
Good Heavens! = surprising

Ouch! That hurts!

— after sentences which express surprise, anger, etc: ▶   What a funny place to put a cucumber!

Use inverted commas
— to mark off direct speech: ▶   'I want you,' he said, 'to make up a story about a dishonest lawyer and a blind chicken.'

— when you are quoting something: ▶   People call him 'The Cisco Kid'.
She's full of 'joie de vivre'.

— to show that you are using a word in a special, unusual way: ▶   She's the real 'boss' in this place.

22.4 The hyphen

You should use the hyphen [-]
— in compound adjectives with *well-*
and *badly-*:

▶   well-dressed, badly-spoken

— in the pattern adj + noun -*ed*:

▶   blue-eyed, long-haired, flat-chested, open-minded,
single-handed

— after prefixes *co-*, *pre-*, *re-*
if it will make the word easier to
recognise:

▶   re-enter (*easier than* reenter)
co-operate (*easier than* cooperate)

Some compound nouns can be
hyphenated, but there are no fixed
rules. If a compound noun is made
up of two short words, and is a
very common one, write it as one
word:

▶   bedroom, policeman, armchair, bookcase, typewriter,
screwdriver

In all other cases, or when you are not
sure, write the compound noun as two
words without a hyphen

▶   dining room, steam engine, vacuum cleaner, petrol station

22.5 The apostrophe

Use the apostrophe
— in verb short forms (See 8.6):

▶   John's got a cold.
He couldn't go to work.

— in the possessive form (See 1.5):

▶   a child's toy
in two years' time

— to show that letters are missing from
a word or phrase:

▶   B'ham for Birmingham
three o'clock

22.6 Capital letters

The personal pronoun *I* is always
written as a capital letter.
The first letter of the following should
also be a capital letter:
— the beginning of each sentence:

▶   Ladies and gentlemen, welcome! We are very pleased to
see you all.

— the names of particular people,
places and things:

▶   Mary, Mr Smith, the United Kingdom, the Times

— the titles of particular people:

▶   Mr, Mrs, Miss, Ms, the Duke of York, Princess Diana, the
President

— days, months and the names of public holidays:

▶ Monday, Tuesday, Wednesday, Thursday, Friday, Saturday, Sunday
January, February, March, April, May, June, July, August, September, October, November, December

New Year's Day, Good Friday, Easter, May Day, Christmas Day, Boxing Day

— nationalities:

▶ the English, Germans, an Italian, the Arabs

— nationality adjectives:

▶ This is a Swiss watch.
I am learning French.

In the titles of plays, books, films, etc, the important words are written with a capital letter:

▶ The Taming of the Shrew
Making Sense of English Grammar
The Good, the Bad and the Ugly

23 Grammatical endings: pronunciation and spelling

23.1 Pronunciation of -s/-es ending

Pronounced [z] after:

[b]	rubs	[rʌbz]	tubes	[tju:bz]
[d]	reads	[ri:dz]	hands	[hændz]
[g]	begs	[begz]	dogs	[dɒgz]
[v]	lives	[lɪvz]	wives	[waɪvz]
[m]	seems	[si:mz]	homes	[həʊmz]
[n]	runs	[rʌnz]	sons	[sʌnz]
[ŋ]	sings	[sɪŋz]	songs	[sɒŋz]
[l]	tells	[telz]	miles	[maɪlz]

And after vowel sounds, eg:

[i:]	agrees	[əˈgri:z]	trees	[tri:z]
[ɑ:]	debars	[dɪˈbɑ:z]	cars	[kɑ:z]
[ə:]	refers	[rɪˈfə:z]	brothers	[ˈbrʌðə:z]
[eɪ]	plays	[pleɪz]	days	[deɪz]

Pronounced [s] after:

[p]	hopes	[həʊps]	lips	[lɪps]
[t]	waits	[weɪts]	cats	[kæts]
[k]	likes	[laɪks]	books	[buks]
[f]	laughs	[lɑ:fs]	beliefs	[bɪˈli:fs]

Pronounced [ɪz] after:

[s]	kisses	[ˈkɪsɪz]	faces	[ˈfeɪsɪz]
[ʃ]	wishes	[ˈwɪʃɪz]	dishes	[ˈdɪʃɪz]
[tʃ]	catches	[ˈkætʃɪz]	matches	[ˈmætʃɪz]
[ks]	fixes	[ˈfɪksɪz]	boxes	[ˈbɒksɪz]
[z]	rises	[ˈraɪzɪz]	sizes	[ˈsaɪzɪz]
[dʒ]	alleges	[əˈledʒɪz]	edges	[ˈedʒɪz]

23.2 Pronunciation of -*d*/-*ed* ending

Pronounced [*d*] after:

[b]	rubbed	[rʌbd]
[g]	begged	[begd]
[v]	lived	[lɪvd]
[m]	seemed	[siːmd]
[n]	signed	[saɪnd]
[ŋ]	ringed	[rɪŋd]
[l]	peeled	[piːld]
[z]	pleased	[pliːzd]
[dʒ]	alleged	[əˈledʒd]

And after vowel sounds, eg:

[iː]	agreed	[əˈgriːd]
[ɑː]	debarred	[dɪˈbɑːd]
[əː]	referred	[rɪˈfəːd]
[eɪ]	played	[pleɪd]

Pronounced [*t*] after:

[p]	hoped	[həʊpt]
[k]	liked	[laɪkt]
[f]	laughed	[lɑːft]
[s]	kissed	[kɪst]
[ʃ]	wished	[wɪʃt]
[tʃ]	watched	[wɒtʃt]
[ks]	fixed	[fɪkst]

Pronounced [*ɪd*] after:

[t]	waited	[ˈweɪtɪd]
[d]	intended	[ɪnˈtendɪd]

23.3 Doubling the consonant

If a word ends in a single vowel + a
single consonant, double the consonant
before adding the endings -er, -est, -ed,
-ing, -y: ▶

single vowel	single consonant	eg	
	b	rub	rubbed
	d	sad	sadder
a	g	big	biggest
	l	fulfil	fulfilled
e	m	hum	hummed
i	n	sun	sunny
o	p	tap	tapping
u	r	prefer	preferred
	t	fat	fatter

Note: there are some exceptions to this
rule, usually when the last syllable of a
word is unstressed, eg: ▶

OFFer   OFFered   OFFering
COMMon COMMoner COMMonest

If you double the consonant, the vowel
sound changes. Compare these pairs
of words: ▶

ride	[raɪd]	rid	['rɪd]
riding	['raɪdɪŋ]	ridding	['rɪdɪŋ]
hoped	[həʊpd]	hopped	[hɒpt]

23.4 Changing -y to -i-

If a word ends in a consonant + y,
change the y to i before adding -es, -er, -
est,
-ed or -ly: ▶

baby	babies
sticky	stickier
lady	ladies
deny	denied
happy	happily
try	tried
easy	easily
lazy	laziest

Similarly, change y to i before adding
such endings as -ful, -less and -ness: ▶

beauty	beautiful
penny	penniless
lonely	loneliness

23.5 Dropping final -e

When a word ends in a consonant + *e,*
— drop the -*e* before adding -*ing*: ▶

bore	boring
owe	owing
serve	serving
use	using

— add only -*d, -r, -st*: ▶

bore	bored	
owe	owed	
nice	nicer	nicest
brave	braver	bravest

Note the verbs *agree* and *see*: ▶

agree — agreeing — agreed
see — seeing

Note also words ending in -*ible*
and - *able:* ▶

terrible	terribly
capable	capably

Index